PLAY BETTER GOLF
WITH PETER ALLISS

Published by BBC Books,
a division of BBC Enterprises Limited,
Woodlands, 80 Wood Lane, London W12 0TT

First published 1989
Reprinted 1989

ISBN 0 563 21429 5 paperback
ISBN 0 563 21442 2 hardback

Set in 11 on 13 pt Sabon monophoto
Printed and bound in Great Britain by Butler & Tanner Ltd, Frome, Somerset
Colour origination by Technik Litho Plates Ltd., Berkhamsted
Colour printed by Lawrence Allen, Weston Super Mare, Avon
Jacket and cover printed by Fletchers, Norwich

in collaboration with Bob Ferrier

edited by Gordon Menzies

BBC BOOKS

CONTENTS

Picture credits

All colour photographs by PHIL SHELDON except for:
BBC/PHIL SHELDON page 65 bottom and cover photographs; KEITH HAILEY SPORTS PHOTOGRAPHIC page 70.
All black and white photographs BBC/PHIL SHELDON except for:
PUNCH pages 9, 32, 56, 98.

All diagrams by GARY REES

Acknowledgement

The words from 'The Charm of Golf', copyright A. A. MILNE, are reproduced with the kind permission of Curtis Brown, London, on behalf of the author's Estate.

FOREWORD BY SEAN CONNERY

My family, my country, my profession and golf – I love them all. Sometimes they vary in order of preference according to who has done what and with which and to whom! For all that I consider myself to have been a very lucky man.

I came to the game of golf late and sometimes I feel just a wee bit jealous when I see young boys and girls in St Andrews, Troon or North Berwick with half a dozen clubs in a little canvas bag, hurrying down to play on these marvellous courses in majestic settings. Part of my jealousy may be that I suspect many of them play a much better game of golf than I do.

In every respect I have been very lucky with the game. It has enriched my life. I have been able to play all over the world and on many of the greatest courses.

They say a late convert is always the most passionate and, since many of my friends do on occasions accuse me of being passionate about the game, I have to plead guilty to that.

Peter Alliss may be partly to blame for that deep passion. I first met him at the Parkstone Golf Club long, long ago, when he was the professional there, and I have enjoyed his friendship and success as a television commentator, writer, teacher and enthusiast ever since.

The BBC-2 Pro-Celebrity Golf Series gave me the opportunity to play with and talk to many great champions; players like Lee Trevino, Sandy Lyle, Greg Norman and many others. I discovered a few things that these great champions have in common. In making the swing they hit the ball very hard, the face of the club is squared up at impact and they stay on balance throughout their swing. They all practise very hard and very seriously. Apart from that, as golfers they don't have very much in common. They all seem to swing the club differently except for that magical two or three feet through the hitting area.

I must come to the conclusion that in this fascinating, frustrating game there is no such thing as the 'universal perfect swing'. There is a perfect swing for me and a perfect swing for you. You can find your perfect swing by getting a few fundamentals right and you can retain its shape, and make it repeat time and time again only by constant practice! If you want to play the piano like Horowitz or if you prefer Oscar Peterson, it's easy, all you have to do is practise eight hours a day for 20 years! So let's face it, we all have to practise.

Peter Alliss, like his famous father Percy, has always maintained that golf is a simple game and should be taught simply. He has done just that in this book. He has looked plainly at the fundamentals of grip, stance, backswing, etc., which all have to be mastered, and has written simply about them. If you read, inwardly digest and practise, you will play better golf.

Good luck.

Tiresome Golf Enthusiast: 'Then observe the absorbing interest of the game, the rhythm of the swing and follow through, the nice adjustment of the approach, the careful choice of line for the putt. Each shot a problem and spur to the intellect. Small wonder that golf has so great a following. Er – what made you take it up?'
Fed-up Colonel: 'Liver.'

Golf is so popular simply because it is the best
game in the world at which to be bad. . . .
At golf it is the bad player who gets the most
strokes.

A. A. Milne

'The Charm of Golf'

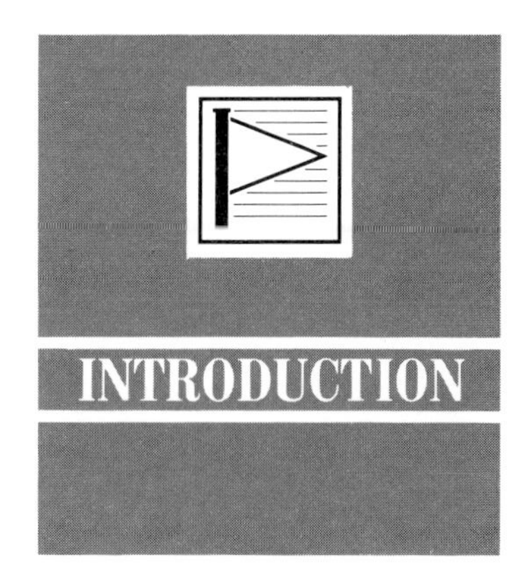

INTRODUCTION

Do you sincerely want to be a better golfer?

If you do, and I assume you do since you have this book in your hands, there are two things you must accept without reservations: you must think about your game, and you must work, that is, practise. If you are not prepared to do both of these, you will never be a better golfer and it may be time to think about snooker or bowls or bridge or chess or the cultivation of roses.

I do lots of 'company days' up and down the country when I go along to a golf course 'hired' for a day by the company concerned. Before lunch I demonstrate some shots, talk of the swing and how to play the game. Then I play a few holes with each group of company guests in the afternoon. Most times I make a golf-oriented speech after dinner and conduct a question-and-answer session afterwards. The sponsoring company uses such a day as a sales incentive for staff, sales reward, promotional or public relations exercise involving either the company's staff or important business clients. All of the people concerned are clearly alert, intelligent and successful.

But when I see them on the golf course, with a golf club in their hands, I am appalled. They seem to have no idea of what they are doing, no particular thought as to how they should stand, how they should grip the club or any idea of rhythm or balance. They make the most fearful lunges at the ball which can fly anywhere, and most of the time it does.

Of course, if someone plays golf only three or four times a year, this is understandable – they will never play well. But even some of these people I meet who tell me they play about 50 times a year really don't have a clear idea of what they are doing. For example, we might come to a short hole of say 190 yards, and I'll say to my group, 'What do you think of club selection here?'. Almost certainly one of them will say, quick as a flash and brimming with confidence, 'A 4-iron' – and he can't even reach 190 yards with his driver! Golfers are not rational beings, it seems. I'm sure it has never occurred to that man to find a quiet corner of his home course and hit a few 4-iron shots, comfortably and with a nice rhythm, to pace out just how far his best 4-iron shot will travel. Then, next time on the golf course, he would know.

The carelessness of golfers fascinates me. I see them arrive on the first tee wearing fashionable clothes, gloves, shoes, caps, with expensive equipment tucked into handsome golf bags. They haven't played for perhaps weeks but, without taking a practice swing, much less hitting a few warm-up shots on the practice ground or even into a net, they step up to the ball and, as I say, make the most terrifying lunge at it. They've no idea about grip, stance, posture, balance, rhythm and they skull the ball almost anywhere. Golf is simple, but 'simple' doesn't mean 'easy'. In fact, it is quite difficult to swing the club correctly and repeatedly. All right, I accept that you want to become a better golfer so from now on we shall think positively and we'll assume that you will make a positive effort to improve.

Golf is the simplest of games, yet one full of the most profound pleasures. It is played outdoors and over natural terrain. It can be played by the golfer alone. It can be played with one, two or three friends, or against 50 or 100 other players in a club competition. It can be played at the time of a golfer's choosing. He is not restricted to a stadium, or the confines of a court, not dependent on other team members, not restricted by time. It is not a violent sport, not a physical contact sport. Its ultimate pleasure lies in the fact that it can never be conquered. The very greatest of champions have all felt that they could have done it, somehow, a little better. Another of its sublime pleasures is hitting the perfect shot, making a correct swing and correct impact at speed, and seeing the ball fly exactly as you had planned it to the precise point on the course to which you wanted to send it. Even the most expert golfers will say that they will not accomplish that more than a few times in the course of a round. But it is an experience that comes to every golfer – you and I can hit the perfect shot and the more we play and practise, the more often we are likely to do it! One thing to appreciate very quickly is that there is no such thing as 'The Perfect Golf Swing'. But there is a perfect golf swing for you, depending on your size, shape and age and so on. This book will help you find it and establish it. Unlike most sports which have the objective of amassing runs, points or goals, golf requires the successful player to hit the ball fewer times than anyone else. However, if the business of swinging the golf club and striking the ball requires a series of very simple physical movements, these have to be co-ordinated. They are compromised, and often made immensely complicated, by the thought processes and inhibitions of the player.

BE PREPARED TO WORK

The game of golf is basically about a man or woman hitting a ball with a stick. The object of the exercise is to strike the ball across country from a teeing ground, and eventually into a hole in the ground measuring $4\frac{1}{4}$ inches. There are 18 such holes in a round of golf and on each hole the distance from the starting point, the teeing ground, to the actual hole-in-the-ground, can vary from 120 yards to as much as 600 yards. The intervening ground can feature a great variety of terrain – sand dunes, heather, bunkers, rough ground, woods, lakes and streams – although a path known as a fairway is cut between each teeing ground and the hole, giving the golfer an inviting route to follow and a target area for the ball, not to mention a comfortable place from which to play the next shot.

These bald and simple facts lead us to realise that the first element in the game which the golfer must recognise and accept is that golf is a point to point game and *not* a game of sheer physical power and distance. The golfer must strike the ball from point A to point B in a controlled manner, so that reaching point B will make it much easier to reach point C. All this is so obvious that golfers too often forget it, or ignore it, particularly those golfers – you've seen them – who smash at the ball as though to send it beyond the blue horizon, often falling over as they do and more often than not hitting the ball into a mass of trouble off the fairway.

What the golfer needs is one unified physical action which will allow him to strike the ball powerfully and accurately. What he needs, in short, is what the great American champion, Ben Hogan, described as 'a correct, powerful and repeating swing'. In this book, I'll be telling you just how to achieve that. But, a word of warning: practise. You will have to be prepared to work at it. Gary Player, a master bunker player, was once chided for being 'lucky' with his shots from the sand. 'Quite right, sir, quite right,' said Player, 'and it's a funny thing – the more I practise, the luckier I get.' A child doesn't learn to walk by thinking about it, or talking about it. It learns by doing it. So be prepared to put some work into your golf. In a strange way, memory is important to the golfer. For any of you who haven't played for some time, your first problem is remembering how you did it last time. So a little golf, a little practice, regularly, is much more profitable than a 'lot' of golf, irregularly.

And one final point: you want to be as good as you can be, in terms of achievement. So take a realistic view of how good, sensibly, you want to be and of what you want from the game. Every golfer has scope for improvement, even Ben Hogan and Gary Player, and a clear, progressive improvement will give you immense pleasure. But you must consider your age, your shape, your height, weight and general physical condition, your flexibility, your desire and, most important, how much time you can give to it. Golf doesn't require the fitness level of Olympic athletes, but you do need enough spring and strength in your legs, for instance, to get you round the 18 holes without stress. That will be perhaps four miles, which is no more than a reasonable stroll for anyone in good health. However, unless you happen to be reading this book at the age of 12, you are not, I must tell you, ever going to be a Sandy Lyle or a Seve Ballesteros. Decide how well you want to play and, if you take my advice and work at the thing, you'll play that well, and perhaps a good deal better. All things being equal, if you read and inwardly digest these words, and think and practise, you can be scoring in the seventies and playing better golf.

Why we are here, what we are talking about and what we are doing is to learn how to strike a golf ball a prescribed distance, in a prescribed direction, accurately and under control. Simple. We want to strike that ball squarely along the target line, the target line being the imaginary line drawn between ball and target. That target may be the flagstick, the green or that point on the fairway where we want the ball to come to rest.

First we had better consider what the golf ball does when it is struck and how it reacts. If we strike the ball squarely and properly, it will fly directly and correctly along that target line. Simple. But if we don't, it won't. Let me amplify this – it is perhaps the most important point for any golfer to know and remember, regardless of his abilities.

The flight of the ball will tell you how the clubface made contact with the ball. Turn that round the other way and it is, of course, equally true – the contact of the clubface on the ball governs its flight path. If the clubface is square to the target line at impact, and the club is swung straight along the target line at impact, the ball will fly straight. That is a fundamental. Accept it, and don't forget it.

There are other things to consider which will affect what we are trying to achieve and which affect the behaviour of the ball: one is the angle of attack (too shallow or too steep) which the club makes on its impact with the ball; another is that the faster the clubhead is moving at impact, the further the ball will fly.

One of the basic problems in the golf swing is that in order to advance the ball the golfer has to stand 'side-on' and contrive to swing his club around him to hit the back of the ball. If you imagine extending our target line backwards from the ball, away from the target, then you have a reference line for the whole business of swinging the club, and for the path and arc of the clubhead with which we hit the ball.

We now have to consider the path of the clubhead. Since the golf swing is an arc, the only possibility of hitting the ball squarely in the back and sending it straight along the target line comes at the bottom of the arc, and then only for an inch or two. Following the line of the arc, the clubhead comes from inside the target line, strikes the ball squarely, then follows on back inside the target line. Thus the perfect swing pattern is *in* to *square* (briefly) to *in* – another fundamental. Accept it, and don't forget it.

Left: the ideal set-up – the square stance

Centre: the closed stance will produce a drawn or hooked shot

Right: the open stance will produce a fade or slice

Thus before we have even picked up a golf club, we have arrived at two critical fundamentals. The ball will do as it is told. It does not have a mind of its own and we tell it what to do with the clubface and the arc of the swing – the direction in which the clubface is pointed at impact, and the direction in which the swing arc is moving at impact.

If you get one of these wrong at impact, your shot will be less than perfect. If you get both wrong, you are compounding the felony. *You* want to dictate to the golf ball. *You* want it to behave exactly as you had planned, in terms of direction and distance, so it is as well to know what happens if you give it the wrong instructions.

If your swing arc is straight along the target line and your clubface is square to that line at impact, you've hit a straight shot. The speed of the clubhead will govern how far the ball will fly. If your swing arc is straight along the target line and your clubface is 'closed' at impact (i.e. pointing to the left of the target line) the ball will *hook*. It will start straight, then curve to the left. If your swing arc is straight along the target line and your clubface is 'open' at impact (i.e. pointing to the right of the target line) the ball will *slice*. It will fly straight, then curve to the right.

If we consider a swing arc moving from inside the target line to outside the target line at impact (in to out) here, too, there are three variations, depending on the clubface at impact: If it points in the same direction as the swing arc, the ball will go straight right – a *push*; If it points to the left of the swing arc, the ball will start to the right, then spin quickly to the left – a *quick hook* ; If it points to the right of the swing arc, the ball will start to the right, then spin quickly further to the right – a *quick slice*. That's the one that, as often as not, goes whistling out of bounds.

Now consider a swing arc moving from outside the target line to inside the target line at impact (out to in). There are three similar variations, depending on the clubface at impact: If it points in the same direction as the swing arc at impact, the ball will fly straight to the left – a *pull*; If it points to the right of the swing arc, the ball will start to the left, then spin

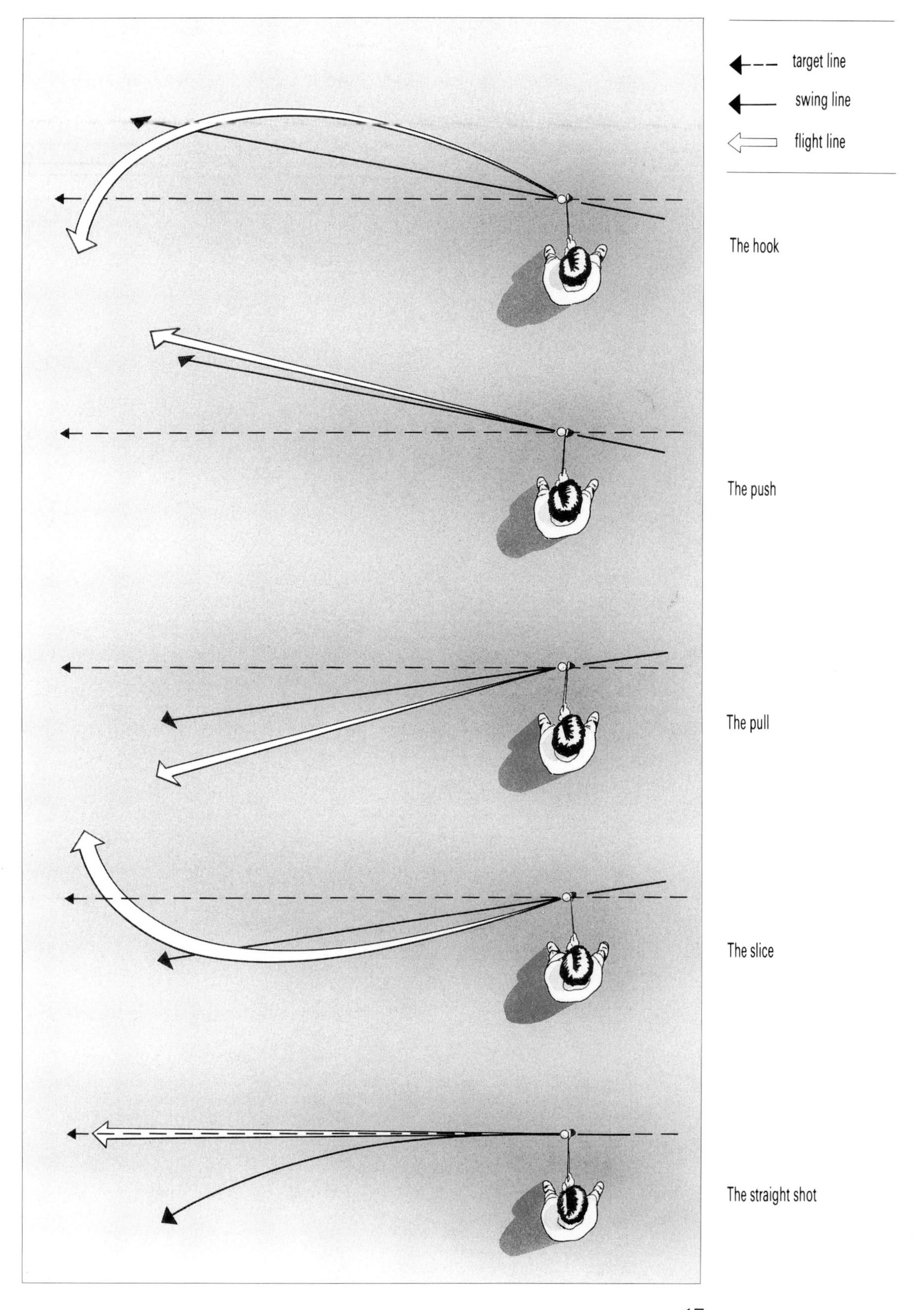
target line
swing line
flight line
The hook
The push
The pull
The slice
The straight shot

Left: the typical slicer's position at impact

Right: the typical hooker's position at impact

quickly and wildly to the right – a *super slice*; If it points to the left of the swing arc, the ball will start to the left, then spin quickly further left – a *smothered hook*.

This ill-disciplined golf ball of ours can misbehave in two other ways. It can pop straight up in the air, going no distance at all – the 'skied' shot – or it can stagger forward without any elevation, without really getting airborne, going no distance at all – the 'skulled' shot.

The first of these means that the clubhead arc has come down too steeply into the lower half of the ball, with the clubface open and with an 'out to in' swing path. The second of these comes from the clubhead rising at impact, and clipping the top of the ball.

You might think that all of this is enough to terrify the Brigade of Guards, but the more I have thought of this game of golf, the more convinced I am that we simply *must* know why the ball behaves as it does when it is struck. We must accept that what we do with the clubface at impact and the path of the swing arc at impact governs absolutely how that impish ball behaves. And we must know all of that if we are to make the ball behave exactly as we want it to behave, to go exactly where we tell it to go, and to be under our control.

Already we have learned some important things about this game. The flight of the ball through the air never lies – it can tell us exactly how it was hit. What's more, golf isn't baseball, isn't a slugger's game – we want to move the ball from precise position to precise position on the course, from point A to point B to point C.

And now we can think of how to do that, by picking up a club, and getting down to work.

THE GRIP

Your hands are your only connection with the golf club. Your hands control the movement of the club and of the clubface, the only part of the golf club which makes contact with the ball, and your hands control every aspect of the golf swing. They must work in unison. Golf isn't tug-of-war. The hands must function throughout the action as one unit and so let us consider the grip, or how the hands should hold the club.

The grip is the first of the basic elements in the golf swing. The others, in sequence, being the stance (and the aim), the backswing, the downswing, the impact and the follow-through. If that looks too much to think about, it isn't. It's a fluid, continuous physical action. After rehearsal and practice, we will scarcely need to think of these things as separate parts.

The grip and the stance are preliminaries. They are in place before any movement starts, so we should be able to get them right. But if you don't get them right, the movement will be wrong and the golf shot will be wrong. So let's get to work, first on the grip.

Bend over slightly from the waist, back straight. Hold your arms out in front of you at an angle of, say, 45 degrees to the ground, with your palms facing each other and touching. Now slide the right hand down the left, away from you, until the tip of the left little finger is touching the bottom joint of the right little finger. By closing your right hand into a fist, right there and still touching your left, you have an idea of how the right hand relates to the left in the final, completed grip. Incidentally, by sliding your right hand forward, you will have stretched your right arm and your right shoulder will drop slightly. Excellent – just what we want.

Now take the club in your left hand, at the top of the shaft, with the shaft lying across the palm diagonally. The shaft should lie between the bottom joint of the left index finger and just in front of the fleshy butt of your left hand. Indeed, if you crook your little finger round the shaft and hold the shaft with pressure from that finger and from the muscles in the fleshy pad of your left hand, you'll find that you can waggle the club, lift the clubhead and make little swings with that left hand alone. You do not need to grip with the other fingers.

By closing the three other fingers round the shaft firmly, and having the thumb lying straight down the top of the shaft, or very slightly to the right as you look down on it, we have established the required left-hand

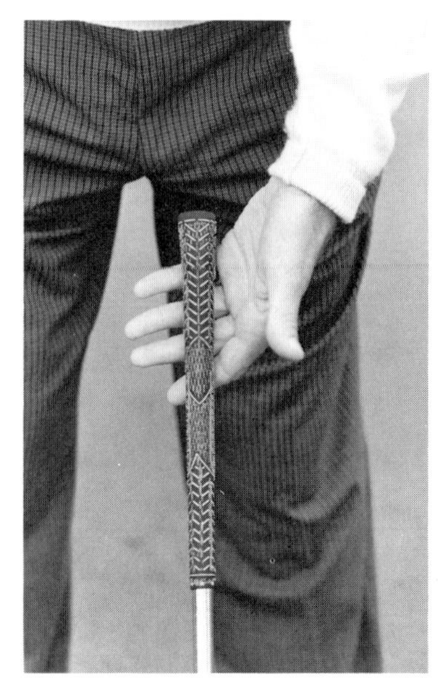

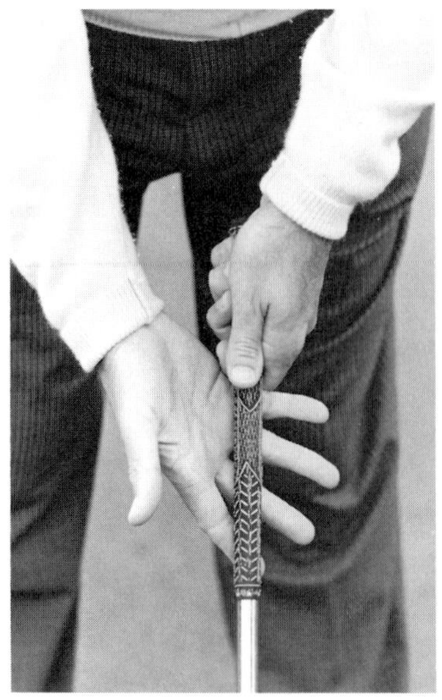

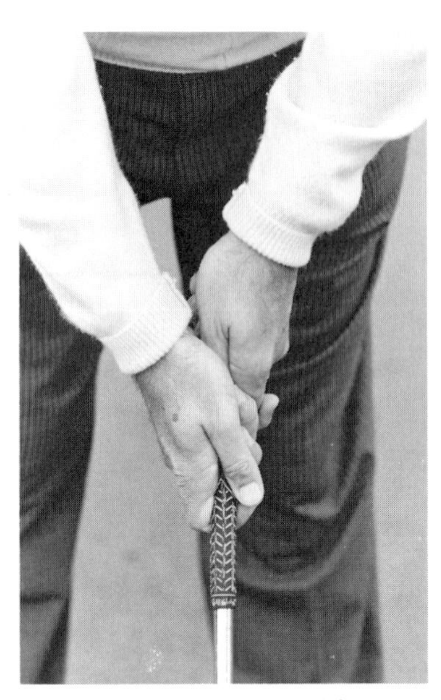

Left: place the club in the left hand

Centre: grip with the left hand and place right hand in position

Right: the completed grip – the 'V' aiming towards the right eye

grip. The 'V' showing between the thumb and index finger should point more or less to the right eye. The left-hand grip is very important – it controls the clubhead and its swing pattern.

In taking up the right-hand grip bring your right hand to the club so that the shaft lies along the bottom joints of your four fingers but not quite in the palm, *below* the palm. Take up a little pressure on the shaft with the two middle fingers of the right hand. Now close all the fingers round the shaft so that the pad at the bottom of your right thumb fits snugly over your left thumb. Close your right thumb and index finger round the shaft. Your right thumb, you will find, lies slightly across the shaft. Pinch the right thumb and index finger together and you will find that the 'V' they make will point towards your right eye, more or less parallel to the 'V' you have already formed with the left thumb and forefinger.

You should next ease your right hand up the shaft so that its little finger rides over the index finger of the left hand. It can rest on top of that finger, hook round it, or lie between it and the next left-hand finger – whichever is more comfortable for you. You have now established a positive hold on the club which will allow you to deliver the face of the club squarely to the ball at impact, provided you are swinging along the correct target line.

I have gone into this in some detail because the grip is really the first fundamental in playing this game. If the grip is wrong, nothing else will be right. In fact, even if you are not an absolute beginner and have played the game for a year or two, it will pay you dividends to review your grip. Even with this, *practice* is the thing – five minutes a day for a couple of weeks, at home and preferably in front of a mirror, will get you into the habit of instinctively taking up your correct grip.

Come to think of it, even if you have been playing the game for as long as ten years you must review your grip constantly – in fact with every single shot! The grip is so fundamental that I would guess that three out

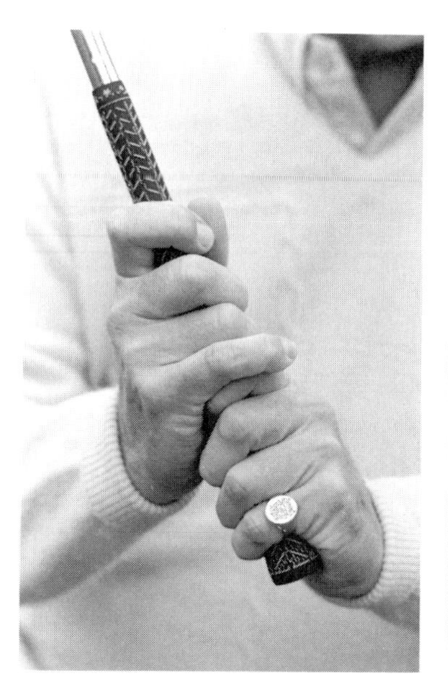

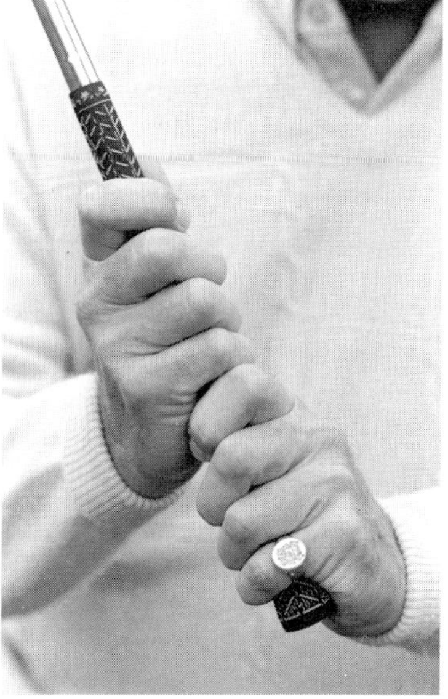

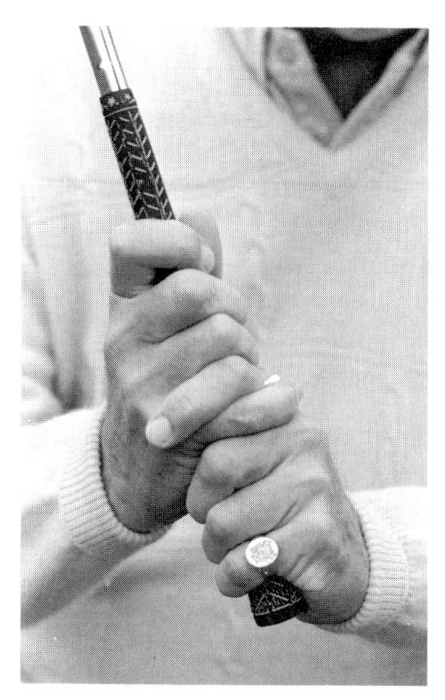

Left: the Vardon or overlapping grip

Centre: the two-handed grip

Right: the interlocking grip

of every four mishit shots are caused by errors in the grip, in not having it quite right at impact.

The grip I have described is the famous and widely-accepted Vardon grip, developed by Harry Vardon from Jersey, who won six Open Championships on either side of the turn of this century and a US Open Championship. There are three basic golf grips, the other two are simple variations on the Vardon, and you can experiment with them all until you are satisfied as to what is best for you. The others are the Interlocking grip and the Baseball grip and they are what they say they are. The Interlocking has the little finger of the right hand entwined with the index finger of the left. This may be a better grip for golfers with small hands – Jack Nicklaus uses it. The Baseball grip has all the fingers of the right hand on the shaft, with the hands just touching – the Ryder Cup golfer and captain, Dai Rees, who played tournament golf successfully into his sixties, and Bob Rosburg, a US PGA Champion, used this grip.

The important thing is that the hands should work in unison. Once you have established your grip on the club, before the swing starts, you *must not* allow it to change. There must be no movement of the shaft in the fingers, and no change in the pressure of the fingers. How firmly should you hold the club? I can't tell you, except to say that the pressure of your grip should be just enough to keep the club under control.

I can tell you what *not* to do – don't hold the club fiercely in a matter-of-life-or-death grip. That will only tighten up the muscles of your arms and inhibit your swinging action. In any case, there will probably be a slight and instinctive tightening of your grip as the clubhead contacts the ball. The grip should be light but positive. Again, Bobby Jones and Ben Hogan, both great champions, believed that the firmest pressure in the golf grip should be applied with the last three fingers of the left hand. You might think of these as the weakest of all ten fingers. The best guidance I can give you is to think of gripping the club with the kind of pressure you

Getting your hands in front of the clubhead – with longer shots – will result in topping the ball

would apply to the steering wheel of a car, in traffic.

Practise the grip. Study it from above, looking down on it. Get it right. Waggle the club – you can do it discreetly at home – to get the feel of the thing, the most comfortable pressure on the thing. And it would not hurt to strengthen your fingers. You can do that simply by squeezing a squash ball, or even a golf ball. Another good exercise is to hold a club at arm's length in your fingers: begin at the top of the grip and slowly turn the club in your fingers working your way down to the bottom of the grip. Stop when it feels sore!

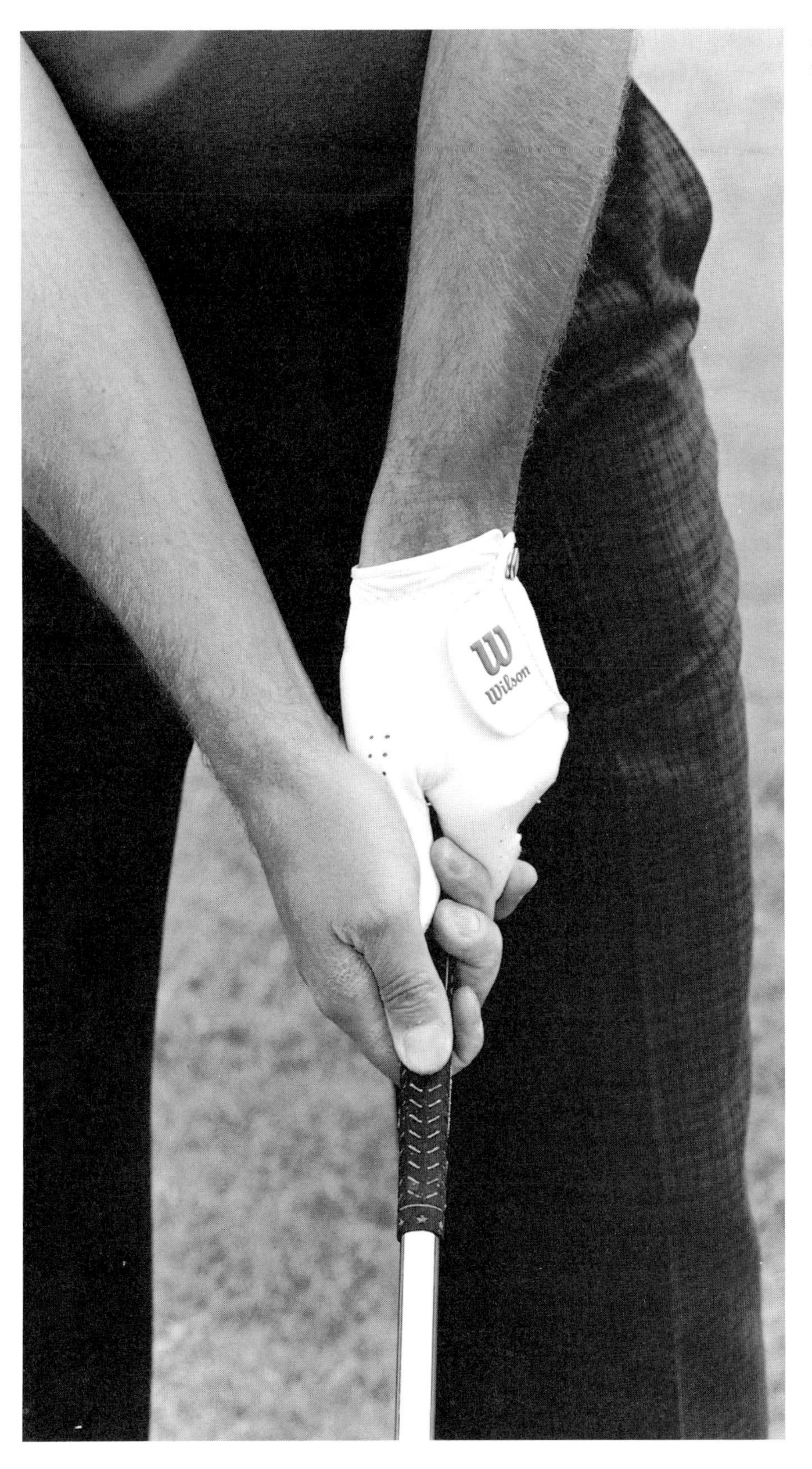

A hooker's grip – and some are worse than that!

Incidentally, as you look down at your hands set round the club in the Vardon grip, you will see two knuckles of the left hand. That is a correct grip. With this grip, if you set the clubface behind the ball, square to the target line before you start any movement, your swing – all other things being equal – will return that clubface square to the ball at impact.

However, if looking down at the grip both hands are turned clockwise on the club so that three or more knuckles of the left hand are showing, with the right hand moving under the shaft – the 'strong' or hooker's grip – the clubface (again, all other things being equal) will return to the ball closed, and you'll be looking at a hooked or smothered shot.

Conversely, as you look down at your hands and turn them anti-clockwise, so that only one left-hand knuckle is showing and the right hand is over the top of the shaft – the 'weak' or slicer's grip – the clubface (again, all other things being equal!) will return to the ball open, and you'll be looking at a vintage slice.

The correct grip puts you in control of the clubface and the clubhead. In the golf swing it allows you to give commands to the clubhead at critical points in the swing – the first movement away from the ball, the top of the backswing and impact.

Many good golfers play with a suspect grip – usually the 'strong' grip with the right hand too much under the shaft. They play well for a time but under pressure (such as requiring a par four on the closing hole to win the medal) it lets them down. How often have you seen such a grip hooking out of bounds.

The grip is item one in the whole procedure – *get it right!*

THE STILL, SILENT CENTRE

The golf swing is one continuous physical movement. It lasts only a few seconds. It does not require much in the way of muscle power but it does require a fluid movement of all the parts of the body with one singular exception. That exception is keeping the head *still*!

The swing demands action and reaction, and this requires above all else a rhythmic movement at a sensible tempo which will maintain the body in balance, prevent it from swaying in any direction, indeed prevent it from falling over. In simple terms, what the golfer must do is swing the club away from the ball, take it round and up to shoulder level or slightly higher – whatever feels comfortable. Then he must reverse the process, react to that process if you like, by bringing the club back down and through the ball to hit it forward. To do this, he will have to turn his torso to the right, assisting the swing of his hands and arms, then bring it all back again – the first turn to the right, the second turn back to the left. In doing all this, he will turn his shoulders to the right a fair way, then turn them back (reaction again) to where they were at address and beyond as the force of the swing carries his upper body round until it is facing down the target line, after the ball has gone.

To do all this successfully, the golfer must stay in *balance*, must stay 'centred' – he must cultivate the *still, silent centre* of the swing. This brings us into the realms of the old golfing sayings, 'Head down', 'Head still', 'Keep your eye on the ball'. All of these have enough truth to be very important. If you are trying to hit something, for example, and don't look at it, you'll have a poor chance of succeeding, whether it is a golf ball, a football, or a nail. Throughout the swing, you must *look* at the ball.

In swinging the club back, you will be rotating the upper body around the spine, which is inclined forward. The human body being what it is, the shoulders can rotate further than the hips. Somewhere at the top of the spine, at the back of the neck is the core, the hub, the fixed point, to which all the movements will relate. It is the 'still spot'. Keeping this spot still is what we are really saying when we talk about keeping the head still. By doing just that we allow the body to turn, perfectly balanced and not moving forwards or backwards, not swaying to right or left, allowing the arms to give us the widest and truest arc with the clubhead. If the golfer moves his head with the backswing, that is to his right, his balance is in

The head must remain still throughout the swing until the follow-through brings it up naturally

danger. On the downswing, when trying to move his head back to its original place, he'll likely over-compensate and hit the top of the ball (assuming he makes any contact with it). If he moves his head to the left at the start of the backswing, the reverse will be true, and he'll likely strike the ground behind the ball.

If a footballer, either rugby or soccer, is kicking a penalty shot right-footed, he will run up to the ball and plant his left foot level with the ball and quite close to it. This gives him his point of balance, allowing his right foot to make a back lift, forward swing, impact and follow-through while he looks at the ball with his head still and stays in balance. The golf swing is no different.

Some people will say that within the physical exertions of the golf swing, the head will move, almost imperceptibly. Maybe it does. *Forget it*! Keep your head still! That point at the back of the neck is the one part of your body that *does not* move in the whole swinging, rotating, up-and-down-and-through sequence of the correct, balanced, golf swing.

And when you come to make that swing, it could well be your only thought.

Well-meaning Caddie: 'I can put you right, Miss, but, understand, you'll 'ave to surrender yerself to me absolootly.'

AIM, STANCE AND POSTURE

The word stance in golf simply means how we set our body in relation to the ball as we make ready to hit it. So it involves posture and taking aim. Taking up your best possible stance gives you the best possible chance of swinging the club effectively along your target line. It involves a good deal of preliminary movement, of shuffling the feet around and so on, until we feel we are in the best and most comfortable position from which to make the swing.

Watching expert players go through this procedure is fascinating. Severiano Ballesteros, for instance, preparing to play an iron shot, will fidget around with his feet and his grip. What he is doing is getting himself into position to produce the particular shot he has in mind – high, low, faded, drawn, whatever. This is altogether too sophisticated for you at the moment, but essentially Ballesteros is doing what all of us must do – putting the body into a correct starting position for the physical action that is to follow. Peter Oosterhuis is another expert player who fidgeted and waggled on the tee, so much so that there were times when I thought he'd never start the swing. But he was the dominant player in European golf in the seventies. You, too, should have a set procedure for taking your stance. As in everything else, habits are important in golf – the good ones, not the bad ones!

First, you grip the club correctly, with the grip you have established is correct for you. Next, you aim the club correctly by placing it behind the ball with the bottom edge of the clubhead at right angles to the target line you have chosen. Finally, you arrange your body relative to that clubface. The object of the exercise, which I can't repeat often enough, is to get your various body parts – hands, arms, shoulders, hips, legs, feet – into positions from which you will be able to make the most effective swing through the ball along the target line, with *control* and in *balance* throughout the entire operation.

In the golf swing, you will be asking certain muscles to function progressively and generate the energy needed to strike through the ball. By putting everything into position before you start, you will make it easy for the muscles to do just that.

Peter Thomson, the great Australian champion who won the Open Championship five times, and who insisted that the golf swing must be a

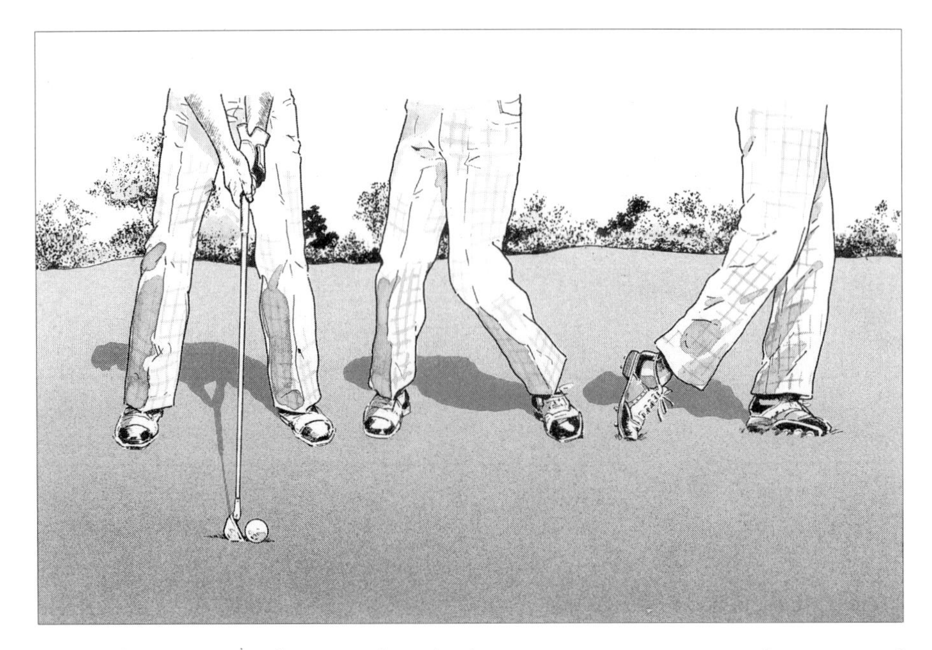

Stay relaxed at address and throughout the swing

simple business, used to say that the best way to set up a good stance and address position was to think of the position you wanted to be in at impact. That is almost absolutely true, except that the stance is more or less static, while the impact position involves fast movement of the hands and arms and of the legs and lower body.

In putting the clubhead behind the ball square to the target line, we should have given some thought to where we want the ball to go. So the first step is to consider the target, the point on the course where we want the ball to come to rest. Be sensible. Think about this. If there is trouble on the left in the shape of bunkers, trees, water, make your target the right side of the fairway. If the hole is a dog-leg and to the right, play to the left side of the fairway. This will open up the second leg and let you see the green. All this is so obvious that we often forget it.

The most critical factor in taking up a correct stance is positioning the clubface. You *must* set it at right angles to your target line, with the sole of the club flat on the ground. Your left arm should be straight, making a straight line from left shoulder through left arm through the club shaft, to the ball. This does *not* mean that the arm will be *stiff*. It should not be locked at the elbow and particularly not at the wrist, which is a hinge we'll be using in the swing. But looking down on the shaft and left arm, we should see a straight line.

Since we are going to strike the ball from the side, rather than from directly behind, it is essential that the clubface and everything else – shoulders, hips, feet – are squared at right angles to that target line. With that in mind we stand at the ball with our feet comfortably apart, about shoulder width or slightly more for the wooden clubs, knees flexed as though we had eased down on to a high stool, back straight but upper body inclined forward from the waist, everything easy and relaxed. Tension of any kind is the enemy of the golf swing.

A useful analogy for getting set is to imagine that you are standing on one railway line, with the ball on the other, and everything else is squared up. The fact that your right hand is gripping the club below your left means that your right shoulder has gone down. *It must not go forward.* Left shoulder up, right shoulder down is fine at address but if you let your right shoulder go forward, i.e., opening the upper half of your body to the line, then you've made the first step towards an out-to-in swing path, and a sliced shot. By the way, both elbows should be nicely tucked in, close to the body, left elbow pointing to left hip, right elbow bent towards the right hip.

Left: the relationship of the feet to the ball with three different clubs: (from outside) a driver; 5-iron; and 9-iron

Right: all shots should be played with the ball just inside the left heel

So now we know what to do, let's do it. Place the clubhead behind the ball. Take aim, so that the clubface is at right angles to the target line. Make sure everything else is too – feet, hips, shoulders. The knees will be flexed comfortably, the back will be straight, inclined forward from the waist, the hand nicely clear of the thighs, giving us room to swing the club through the ball.

Address the ball with an easy, relaxed posture

Ball position? A point opposite the inside of the left heel, but certainly forward of centre. The reason is that on the downswing, with the legs driving forward, the bottom of the swing arc will flatten for an inch or two before and after impact, so that the ball is hit neither upwards nor downwards but forwards. The angle of the face of the club (loft) will make the ball airborne. Remember that even a driver has some loft.

Now some reservations: no two golfers stand exactly alike or swing exactly alike and I have definite opinions on the setting of the feet, and of the ball position, which might help you.

Sir Henry Cotton, three times Open Champion, used to stand with his feet resolutely square to the target line – Henry was rather pigeon-toed. Ben Hogan had his right foot square to the target line and his left foot turned slightly towards the hole. He felt that a square right foot prevented him from turning his right hip too far round on the backswing and also prevented his right leg from moving or swaying to the right as his backswing was being completed.

My own feeling is that the feet should not be rigidly square to the target line, but that the toes should be turned outwards slightly, as in 'five to one' on a clockface. All things considered, I believe this foot position makes it easier for you to turn, and to come back through to sweep the ball forward and away from you. At the same time, the left foot can be slightly withdrawn, an inch or two from the target line. That too can help you sweep the ball away. I am not suggesting that your entire left side should be 'open' pointing to the left of the target line – just an inch or two.

I believe that the ball position we have established, more or less opposite or just inside the left heel, should remain there for *all* your shots as you work through the bag from driver to pitching wedge. As the shots get shorter, the right foot should simply move closer towards the left, narrowing the stance, as we say. (This applies to everything except the 'specialist' shots, i.e. bunker shots, or shots from deep rough or difficult lies, etc.)

As the clubs become progressively shorter in the shaft and more lofted in the face, the swings needed for each of them will also be progressively shorter. In fact, I would say it is almost impossible to have too narrow a stance – when we get down to playing little pitch and chip shots from just off the green the feet are quite close together. When Bobby Jones was playing these shots his feet were almost touching. On the other hand, you can certainly have too wide a stance, one that prevents you from making any sensible hip turn.

I am a strong believer in keeping that ball position constant for all the orthodox shots. For one thing, it will keep your body weight behind the ball and behind the shot at the moment of impact, which is what you want. And it is a good deal simpler than having that extra burden of considering a new ball position for every club in your bag.

The fact that the right hand is under the left when you grip the club has eased the right shoulder lower than the left, as we have seen. That, plus the fact that you are set up with a straight left arm and straight shaft, running down to the ball from the left shoulder, will keep your head behind the ball, which is also what we want.

So the whole business of the set-up – aim, posture, stance – means being relaxed, comfortable, ready and in the right body position to start the dynamic action of taking the club back, then making a correct, balanced and powerful sweep through the ball.

THE FIRST CRITICAL POINT:

THE START OF THE BACKSWING

We have checked through the preliminaries to the golf swing: how to grip the club correctly; how to take a proper stance in relation to the ball and so to 'aim' the shot; and we have accepted that a still head will provide the hub, and indeed the one fixed reference point for all the action to come.

Now we are ready to consider movement, actually swinging the clubhead. But before we get to the first critical point in the swing – the start of the backswing – it might be useful if I remind you that the object of this entire exercise is to help you get that club to a point from which you will be able to make a correct and reliable downwards swing, to and past the ball, and so play better golf. We will be discussing the separate portions of the complete swing, so that you will be able to apply them in sequence (and understand why we do one thing and not the other). If you do understand all the whys and apply the parts in sequence, and practise, you *will* play better golf.

What we want at the top of the backswing is a balanced and controlled position leading us on to a downswing which will give us a correct and powerful impact with the ball. To get to that balanced and controlled position we are going to draw the clubhead back from the ball and, with hands, arms, shoulders and the turning of the upper body away from the ball, we are going to carry the clubhead back, round and up to that position.

The first movement of the clubhead away from the ball is critical. It will govern the quality and efficiency of all that follows in the swing. After all, it is the very first physical movement we shall make in the swing.

Jack Nicklaus has said, 'It is impossible to be too slow over the first 18 inches of the backswing.' Nicklaus himself is a perfect example of this – his first movement is about as deliberate as you can imagine.

This initial, deliberate movement of the clubhead away from the ball will set the tempo of the swing and the line of the arc of the swing. I suggest you practise it by taking the clubhead back 18 inches, no more, and doing it under the control of your left side. Set yourself up with a proper grip and stance and with the left arm and shaft forming a straight line to the ball. Now take the clubhead back, keeping your left arm straight and without breaking your wrists and keeping your head still. You will find that important things happen quite naturally.

Opposite: analysing Tommy Horton's swing – the start of the backswing

The clubhead will move back inside the target line, and your left shoulder will start instinctively to glide under your chin. The shoulders should rotate, left down, right up, quite naturally. This is marvellous news – we want to make a full shoulder turn to reach eventually that 'balanced, controlled' and powerful position at the top of the backswing, and we are already on the way. Do this a dozen times – obeying my rules – and you will see that it works. I repeat, keep the left arm straight, don't break the wrists, keep the head still and take the clubhead away – it will move inside the target line and the left shoulder will move under the chin, starting a correct rotation of the shoulders. This is the first great revelation in the business of the golf swing.

Something else happens this early. As the left shoulder starts down, the left knee starts to bend slightly. Let it happen. In fact, on the backswing don't worry too much about leg action – they will react naturally to the upper body movement. In the same way, you can forget about your feet. Their business is not action, but reaction.

This initial 'takeaway' of the clubhead sets the tempo of the action, maintains it in control, maintains the golfer's balance and posture, and leaves things co-ordinated. No need for straightening knees, bending elbows, doing anything with legs or feet or wrists.

In fact, the golfer would do well to accept that the essence of the backswing is a progressive coiling of the upper part of the body. The arms and hands control the arc and plane of the swing and direct the clubhead to the ball. But the power of the physical action, transmitted through these arms and hands, comes from the progressive uncoiling of the upper part of the body on the downswing. That's reaction again. The downswing will be a reaction to the action of the backswing.

In continuing this 'mini-swing' backwards other things will happen in sequence. If the golf swing is a matter of actions and reactions, it is also a matter of sequences – one thing follows on from the other – and you must have the patience to allow them to happen.

You will find that as you take the club further back, the left shoulder will slip further under the chin. The left knee will flex a little more and start to move slightly inwards, towards the right. You will have an awareness that your weight is easing over to your right leg and your right hip will begin to move backwards. Let it all happen!

When your hands reach a point somewhere level with your hips, the wrists will want to hinge, or 'cock'. *Let it happen.* This is simply to allow the hands to control and carry the weight of the clubhead as it rises, and help you along the way to making a full shoulder turn. As you go on up to the top of the backswing, keeping the head still, your left heel will ease off the ground and you will have most of your weight on the right foot. In fact, you should feel some tension along the muscles of the inside of the right leg, which is still flexed, *not* straightened. Some top-class players say that they feel 'perched' on their right hip at the top of the backswing.

In going up to the top of the backswing, with the left arm straight, the right elbow will fold in naturally until it is pointing to the ground. At the

top of the swing there should be tension in the muscles of the upper back, the left shoulder and left arm. Our intention will be to turn the shoulders and upper back about 90° to the right. Here we have to be sensible. Some people just cannot turn that far round, because of age, physique or whatever. Turn as far as you comfortably can. Golf isn't supposed to be torture. Of course, it will help if you get these muscles into reasonable condition by some gentle exercise, by simply swinging the golf club. If you are particularly lithe, don't swing more than 90°. The more you 'over-swing', the more you lose control of that clubhead.

In turning the shoulders through 90°, your hips will turn about 45° – they cannot turn any further than that, unless you want to step back a pace with your right foot which is not recommended!

So now we have reached the top of the swing. We have taken the clubhead back slowly from the ball, keeping left-shoulder-arms-shaft-clubhead in a straight line, and keeping the *head still*. We have let the weight ease over to the right side with the right knee nicely flexed. We have allowed the left heel to come off the ground, the left knee to move slightly inwards, and we have let the wrists cock naturally. The right elbow will be pointing downwards and not too far from the right ribcage. And the left shoulder will be under the chin. In a phrase, we have wound up the upper body.

With practice, all of this will become one continuous action, at a tempo which will be comfortable for the individual. Let's face it, some players swing the club faster than others – that's really a matter of temperament. Maybe little fellows do it faster. Ian Woosnam and Manuel Pinero, for example, seem to have brisker swings than, say, Nick Faldo or Sandy Lyle. But you can be sure that when it comes to impact, they all have the clubhead going through the ball at top speed.

There are two main points about the backswing. It is not possible to be too slow on the backswing, and, you don't hit anything on the backswing. If you are too quick, you will lose your balance and, if your lose your balance, you cannot hit a proper golf shot. And since you don't hit anything on the backswing, there is no need to make it violent – a waste of effort and energy!

Completing the backswing takes us to the next critical point in the golf swing: the 'top of the swing' position and it is very, very important!

THE SECOND CRITICAL POINT:

THE TOP OF THE SWING

A correct position at the top of the backswing will (a) prove that you have completed the backswing correctly and (b) leave you in the optimum position from which to make a correct downswing to, and beyond, impact with the ball. This is what the golf swing requires. Get yourself into that correct position at the top and you will feel confident of making a proper swing through the ball.

At the top of the backswing, the shaft of the club should be parallel to the ground, parallel to the target line and pointing towards the target. Your grip of the club is critically important here. The arc of the golf swing means that centrifugal force is being applied at the clubhead. The clubhead will tend to continue on its arc but of course we have to stop it at one point and reverse it, bringing it back down towards the ball. To stay in control of these forces, we must have a positive grip of the club at the top of the swing, just as we had at address, just as we must have throughout the swinging action.

Many golfers, because they have to 'stop' the club at the top and reverse the direction of the swing, lose control. They let the right hand relax and 'open', with the butt of that hand falling away from any contact with the left thumb. Others might relax the left hand slightly and let the shaft slip out of the palm into the fingers. This carelessness is fatal – it means that the relationship of the grip to the clubface (remember we established this before the swing started) will alter. On the downswing it is impossible to retrieve and restore this so the clubface will make a faulty contact with the ball, and will not behave itself. You must be the boss. The clubhead, the clubface, must do what you tell it to do, not what it wants to do.

If you were to stop everything at the top of the swing and hold it there, motionless, you would find after a very few seconds that the golf club seems to weigh a ton, and it becomes quite difficult to hold it there. The fact is that when we bring the hands to a stop at the top of the swing, before starting down again, the clubhead may well still be going back. This is a matter of centrifugal force and the flex in the club shaft. In fact, it is a matter of the laws of physics, not the laws of man. So it might be useful just to pause with the hands, until the clubhead 'comes to rest' as it were, at the top of the swing. In fact, some first-class players let everything come to a dead stop at the top before starting downwards again. Gordon

The top of the swing as demonstrated by Tommy Horton

J. Brand, the successful tournament player, is an outstanding example of the full-stop-and-wait at the top of the swing.

This top of the swing position *must* be in balance, *must* be under tight control, because it leads us into the third critical point of the golf swing!

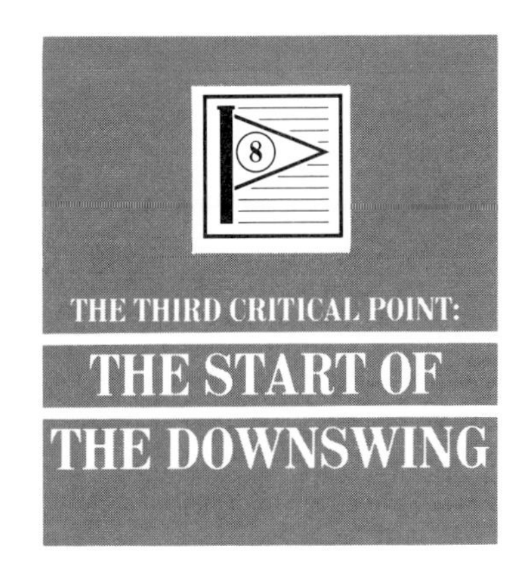

THE THIRD CRITICAL POINT:

THE START OF THE DOWNSWING

I've been going on about these critical points, quite rightly, because they are important. But do remember – they are all parts of a continuous movement. The entire golf swing from beginning to end is a single entity. What I have been doing is listing the pieces of the jigsaw which fit in sequence and when they are all put together you will have a correct and reliable golf swing which can be repeated, time after time. This is what you want. This is what will allow you to play better golf.

If we review your position at the top of the swing, you will remember that by keeping your head still, and with the help of a correct shoulder and hip turn, you have been able to swing the clubhead back and up into a powerful position at the top. In doing this, you have 'wound up' your upper body, coiled it, or if you prefer, compressed it like a spring, with the muscles of the top of the back and left side, shoulders and left arm wound up and ready to supply the power of the swing through the hands and arms.

In the backswing, your lower body – legs and feet – will have been almost passive. In one sense they have resisted the wind-up of the upper body, and so increased the effect of the wind-up. They have been active simply in supporting the turn of the upper body and, when you reach that top position with most of the weight on a firmly planted right foot, you will get strong messages of power and strength from all the muscles along the inside of the right leg. You are ready to go!

Before we start on the downswing, consider again what happened on the upswing. Remember we started with a still head, took the clubhead slowly away from the ball with a straight left arm and, without breaking the wrists, allowed the left shoulder to move under the chin. We allowed the hips to turn, let the wrists cock naturally around hip level and swung the club round and up to that top position.

The one memo that you should send yourself at the top of the swing is that you are going to *swing the clubhead* – you are not going to lift it, drop it, throw it at the ball but swing it back to and through the ball.

The downswing is almost exactly the same sequence as the upswing in reverse. The sequence of the downswing is *feet – legs – hips – shoulders – arms – wrists – hands*. They must all be co-ordinated. The thing must flow. When we get to the impact position we must be like the footballer with his penalty kick – weight on the left foot, his head 'behind' the ball and in balance. So again, with the head still, the feet and the legs start moving on their way to that impact position, and at the same time, the hips start turning back towards the ball. The shoulders start unwinding with the left shoulder going round and up, the right shoulder coming down and going under the chin.

The left knee moves back to its starting position and firms up as it prepares to receive the weight. The right knee, as it surrenders its weight-bearing role, folds in towards the left.

All this time, the hands and arms have been rather left behind. But this turning of the upper body pulls them down, nicely inside the target line. It is important that they are 'left behind'. If the hands and arms get ahead of the unwinding of the trunk all that stored power is lost, squandered.

All this time, too, the wrists remain cocked, as they were at the top of the swing, so that an angle is formed between the left forearm and the club shaft. Just as in the backswing they first cocked on the way up, so on the way down they will uncock at more or less the same point, somewhere around hip level.

It is at this point on the downswing that you should be concentrating on 'releasing' the wrists and making the clubhead whip through the ball. Bobby Jones said that his impression of the golf swing was that he was swinging a weight on the end of a piece of string and that he was making a whipping action through the ball.

Now the upper body has turned, giving the hands and arms room to work as it pulls them down. The legs will be driving forward and your impression will be of a 'swish' through the ball, letting the clubhead accelerate through the ball with your weight almost entirely on your left foot.

The left hand guides the clubhead along the arc of the swing – at the moment of uncocking the wrists the right hand takes a prominent part in the proceedings by adding speed of clubhead to the power created by the unwinding of the upper body. The time and place in the action when this wrist uncocking takes place depends largely on the strength of your wrists, but you mustn't let it happen too soon. Wait for it.

Important things must be said about the downswing. *Start it slowly,* just as you started the backswing slowly. Remember, you can't hit the ball until you get to it – or more precisely, the clubhead can't hit the ball until it gets there. You are swinging the clubhead. The right shoulder must go down and under the chin, not round. If it goes round, and flat, it throws the hands outside the true line of the arc and the clubhead will come from outside the target line, cut across and not through the ball, and you will have guaranteed a sliced shot.

You might want to know that Sam Snead, one of the great champions in the game who hit the ball vast distances, said, 'If I want to hit it further, I swing more slowly'. You are not looking for a fast swing. The only speed needed as such in the golf swing is at the clubhead on impact.

To sum up the downswing then: the lower half of the body (feet and

The downswing as demonstrated by Tommy Horton

legs) starts to turn while the upper half (hips, shoulders, hands and arms) lags behind, in a way almost resisting the action until the golfer's weight is on his left foot. Then hips and shoulders turn, clearing the way for the arms and hands to swing freely, pulling them down at the same time inside the target line, along the correct arc, perfectly on track for the ball. The uncocking of the wrists and a swish of the arms through the ball is the final act in the performance.

These are the fundamentals of the golf swing. Practise them, and they will serve you well. Remember above all that the golf swing is not some machine churning out shots like bottle tops. Some golfers, Ben Hogan for example, have been called 'mechanical men' simply because they have played and practised so much that they hit shot after shot that looked identical. But golf is a game, not an exact science. You must learn, by applying the fundamentals, to swing the clubhead smoothly and precisely, within your own physical capabilities, and the more consistently you do that, the more pleasure you will get from the game.

Know the fundamentals – and apply them!

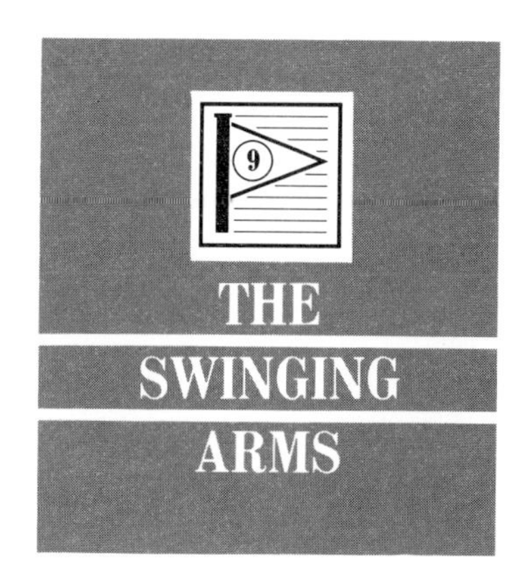

THE SWINGING ARMS

One thing you must have clear in your mind about the golf swing is that it is the arms which swing the club and therefore the clubhead. The hands do *not*. Try this simple exercise. Take up your grip, and stand to an imaginary ball. Now try to swing the clubhead back and forth with the hands, keeping the arms still. You can't. You will move the clubhead only a couple of feet in either direction because the movement is restricted by the degree of hinge in your wrists. You must swing the arms to swing the clubhead.

It can be said that all the body movement in the backswing is done to allow the arms – the left arm in particular – to take the widest possible arc, and all the body movement on the downswing is done to pull the arms through and give them enough space to make a clean, effective swing through the ball. If you make a proper body turn and you have a full, free, rhythmic arm swing, you are well on your way to becoming a very good player.

In fact, it is much more important in the golf swing to think arms instead of thinking hands. On the way back, the hands will cock automatically. If they don't you will never reach a top-of-the-swing position. On the way down, the hands will uncock automatically. They cock and uncock naturally because of the swinging of the arms and the centrifugal force generated at the clubhead. You can almost forget all this – with practice, you will find that it simply happens.

This may surprise many people. Henry Cotton, for example, preached 'hands, hands, hands' as the ultimate key to the golf swing and, as we saw at the very beginning, the hands are your only contact with the club and they control the clubface. That's why, for example, the hands should be alive and well and in control at the top of the backswing, as we have seen. But the fact is that the arms swing with the shoulders – they transmit the power of the turning upper body through the hands to the ball.

Thus one of the common problems with the absolute beginner is a shoulder heave at the top of the swing. It is almost as though he does not have the patience to wait for the clubhead to get to the ball. He throws his upper body at it, spinning the right shoulder round instead of down and under his chin. The result is that the arms are cramped, the arc of the downswing is thrown outside the target line, the clubface reaches the ball on an out-to-in line and cuts across the ball. The shot is sliced or smothered.

Another fault is uncocking the wrists too soon, before nature intended. This simply dissipates the power in the swing long before the clubhead is ready to apply it – at impact.

Please note this about the arms. At any given point in the swing, one of the arms is always straight. Throughout the entire backswing and downswing the left arm is straight, with the right elbow folded inwards. At a point very shortly after impact, with the right hand chasing the ball along the target line, the right elbow will straighten until the right arm is straight at the same time as the left elbow is folding in. The right arm will remain straight more or less until you relax both arms, at the finish of the follow-through.

You have to have an overall conception of the golf swing, in which you visualise that the backswing and top of the swing position have simply compressed all your power, and in releasing it and applying it, the flow of that power goes in the sequence we have listed – legs, hips, shoulders – and flows through the shaft and down to the clubhead from the arms, the swinging arms. If you fix this concept clearly in your mind, and practise, you will be a much better golfer than you think you can be.

But ah, there is much more to this ancient, perplexing game than swinging a club, striking a ball. And that is part of its fascination....

Having discussed the golf swing as a series of movements in sequence, pointing out a few critical points that need particular attention, we now have to put all of these movements together so that we have one continuous flowing action.

We have taken the clubhead slowly away from the ball, completed the backswing slowly, perhaps even paused fractionally at the top of the backswing. We've started the downswing slowly and then made the clubhead accelerate into and beyond impact with the ball. In putting all of this together we have to talk about balance, tempo, rhythm. This takes us into grey areas – these words are difficult to define. It takes us into the realm of the senses, of trying to talk about something which, more accurately, we feel.

Most everyday activities – walking along the street, climbing stairs, getting into and out of a car – find the human body in balance. It all happens, we don't have to think about it. But all this didn't just happen. We didn't have this talent at birth. A baby first starting to walk does not have balance. It falls over. It learns how to stay in balance with practice. The same is true of all human movement, from the simplest action to the most complicated. So the same is true of the golf swing. It needs practice. If the golfer keeps his head still and doesn't swing back too far or too quickly he should stay comfortably in balance.

The quickness of the golf swing, just how quick it should be, puts us into the realm of tempo. One definition of the word is 'the proper or characteristic speed of anything'. I think the key word there is 'characteristic'. Some people are fast movers: they walk quickly, climb stairs quickly. Some people walk deliberately, with a regular, measured gait: others walk slowly. In golf the little fellows, Woosnam, Pinero and before them Dai Rees, seem to be brisk swingers, fast walkers. The bigger fellows sometimes seem more leisurely – Faldo, Lyle and before them Bobby Locke.

The tempo of their physical movement is natural, emerging from their own characters. You have to dig into your own character and extract from it the perfect tempo for you. There is no need to copy anyone. It will emerge from simply swinging the club – from practice.

Rhythm is slightly different. Rhythm is 'movement marked by the regulated succession of strong and weak elements, or of opposite or different conditions'. Pretty good. Or try this one – 'the due correlation and interdependence of parts, producing a harmonious whole.' Ah, that's what we want – a harmonious whole!

You develop a rhythm to go with your tempo by swinging the clubhead backwards and forwards, back and forth, back and forth. Some people have said that repeating the waltz rhythm in their minds has helped with tempo. It is certainly worth a try. You think '*one*, two-three' to take you to the top of the backswing, then '*one* two-three' to take you down, under, and past the ball into the follow-through.

I haven't said much about the follow-through so far. I see a proper follow-through as the logical, inevitable result of a correct swing. But you must complete it. You must allow the clubhead to go through and beyond the ball, following with the hands and arms until it starts to come back inside the target line, as it will. The golf swing does not begin and end with impact. It ends when the clubhead, arms and hands have swung through and up with a firm grip maintained on the club.

One of the golfer's major faults is hitting *at* the ball and not *through* the ball – the equivalent of 'quitting' on the stroke. The final, follow-through position should be just as firm, just as positive, just as balanced, as the top-of-the-backswing position.

Maintaining balance and swinging at your natural tempo with a regular rhythm will give you, with practice, a feeling for your swing, a feeling that it is right. The art of the golf swing is in swinging the clubhead in a controlled manner in your own personal style. If you feel that you are turning your upper body to the right and swinging the clubhead round and up on the backswing; then turning your upper body to the left and swinging the clubhead down, under and through on the downswing, you will have a feeling that you've got the thing right.

This might be a good time to remind you to think about the swing as a whole. The entire golf swing takes only a couple of seconds to complete. You don't have time to think of anything much during the swing. So do your thinking before you put club to ball. Think about where you want it to go. Think about how you are going to strike that ball. Think about the whole swing. Take a couple of practice swings, concentrating on one thing. Take a dozen practice swings if you feel it will help, but remember, the golf course is not the place to put your swing right if it is wrong – the practice ground is the place for that. Remember what the tournament players say about the swing – 'If you don't bring it with you, you won't find it here.'

In any golf club there is never any shortage of advice from members who probably don't know any better, can't play any better, than you. Don't listen – go to your club professional. He knows about the golf swing. It's not just his business to know, it's his life. And he knows you, your age, your physique, the frequency with which you can play. A couple of lessons from him, sensibly applied, will be money in the bank for you!

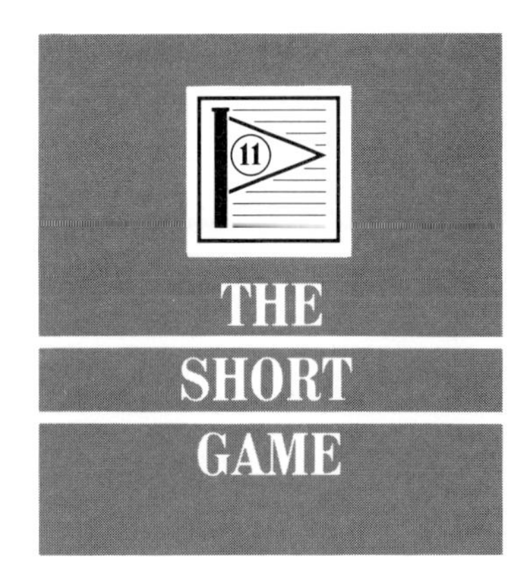

THE SHORT GAME

The green is the end of the line in golf, the arena in which each of the 18 separate dramas in the round takes place. The green is where you are faced with the ultimate objective of the game – getting the ball into the hole.

Before you do that, of course, you have to get there. You have to hit the green from the fairway and, before you get there, you have to drive the ball into the fairway. Every part of the game, then, is important and inter-dependent, but your work on the green is critical. Sam Snead, the American champion, once said that if he had to do it all over again he would practise driving and putting before all else.

The pitch, the chip and the putt comprise the 'short game', and they represent the most expensive item in the golfer's account – here is where he squanders most of his lost strokes. And it is surprising. The shorter shots should be the easiest to play. No physical strength is required. The mechanics are simpler. The two basic rules of golf apply to them as they apply to all golf shots – keep the head still and swing the clubhead.

I suppose the most important factor in playing these shots is judgement: judgement of distance, of where to land the ball and how far it will roll. I cannot teach you judgement, no one can. You must learn it from experience, which means play and practice.

Putting

Since at least half of the strokes you expend in an average round of golf are played on the putting green, the business of putting is certainly worth half of your practice time and half of the total thought you give to the game.

The putting stroke is the golf stroke in miniature. Since the body movement in putting is much reduced, so the emotional element is much increased. The nearer we get to the hole, the more anguished this game becomes! We all know that when we count up our score a two-foot putt has the same value as a 250-yard drive. I know – I've missed too many from two feet!

Bobby Jones has said that on these short putts we find our emotions, our mental processes, switching to 'negative' – we are somehow more concerned with not missing it than we are with holing it. So probably the best advice I can give to anyone faced with any putt, no matter how long,

Her first medal round – *Amelia (to her putter):* 'How can you look me in the face after the way you let me down today?'

how short, how difficult it may be, is to *think positively*. You must convince yourself that you *will* get the ball to the hole. Negative thinking brings tension, anxiety, carelessness.

Jack Nicklaus has said that every golfer should approach every shot with confidence and enthusiasm. Nowhere is this more important than on the greens. The fact is that the shorter the shot, the easier it is to play – *if* you stay relaxed and in control and confident.

The point of this book, as I hope I said at the beginning, is to keep things simple. I will give you a few essentials which will help make you a reliable putter, a player who will seldom take three putts, and one who will get his good share of single putts.

1 You must keep your head still.
2 Every putt is a straight putt.
3 You strike the ball and only the ball.
4 You must accelerate the blade of the putter through the ball.
5 Reach the hole!

These fundamentals need a little explanation. The fact is that with every shot in the game, from long drive to short putt, the head must be kept still. That is a fundamental of golf, which I preach to the point of boredom. More putts have been ruined by head up than by any other single reason. It is simply impatience – looking up to see where the thing is going before you have hit it correctly. You're not likely to lose a ball on the putting green – it won't fly away – so you'd do much better to listen for it rattling into the hole rather than looking for it.

When I say that every putt is a straight putt, I can hear you say, 'rubbish!' But hold on – what I am really saying is that once you have established the line of the putt, the path you want it to follow across the green, you hit the ball directly, straight, along that line. If you have a 40-foot putt and decide that it will break four feet to the left, don't try to turn the ball to the left. Let the slope do it for you. So, you putt the ball along a line four feet to the right of that hole and straight along that line.

If you find it useful to pick an aiming point 12 or 18 inches in front of the ball, use it – hit the ball directly over that point and let the slope take care of the turn. The ball will do as you tell it, just hit it straight.

In considering the putting action you must concentrate on hitting the ball, not the ground between you and the ball, but the ball and in particular the back of the ball. Walter Travis, the American who was Amateur Champion on both sides of the Atlantic early in this century, used to say that in his putting action – he was an outstanding putter – he felt that his right hand was driving a tack into the middle of the back of the ball! So don't stab or stub the shot – hit the back of the ball.

What is an absolute necessity in putting is to *accelerate* the putter face through the ball. This is an essential, like keeping the head still on every shot in golf, but it is critically important in putting. If the putter head is slowing as it reaches the ball, you have lost all control of the ball, you have denied the ball the energy it needs to get to the hole. You may hinge your left wrist backwards in the stroke. You may not hinge it forward on the forward stroke. Practice swings are very useful in this, in establishing the speed you intend to put on the ball, and the fact that your stroke will accelerate through the ball.

This takes me to the last fundamental, that of getting the ball up to the hole. Another Bobby Jones dictum was that the ball which went past the hole would certainly have gone in had we had the line and the direction right, but we can say for certain that the ball which is short of the hole never had any chance of dropping. So try always to get the ball up to the hole. I can't teach you how to do this. No one can. It comes from experience, practice. If you want to imagine that the left hand controls the line of the putt and the right hand the speed, then that might be helpful.

Two things are basic to every putt – the line and the speed of the ball or, if you prefer, direction and weight. Once you have established the path you want the ball to follow and set the blade of the putter at right angles to that path, forget line! Concentrate on making a pure stroke at the ball, accelerating the putter face through the ball. It goes without saying that the blade of the putter must go through the ball absolutely square to the line you have chosen.

As far as the actual stroke is concerned what we want is straight back, straight through. As we have seen, golf is a 'side-on' game, so the clubhead, on longer backswings, will come slightly inside the target line and, once it has gone straight through the ball, will turn back inside the target line. But for a few inches before and beyond impact you must have it going straight.

Once you have decided on the path of the ball, whether it is two feet or 20 feet, you can almost forget it and concentrate on the purity of the stroke. The stroke is the thing in putting and fear is the greatest enemy. The shorter the putt, the more difficult it is to force yourself to 'swing' the clubhead, but swing it you must.

Apart from these fundamentals – another is having your eyes over the ball at address – I'm not sure that putting can be taught in the ordinary sense. It is largely a matter of feel and experience and even inspiration, which means that you must play and practise, play and practise. The more you do it, always bearing in mind these fundamentals, the better you will become.

The grip and the stance for putting can be summed up in a very few words – if they are comfortable and they work, then they are right. One simple thought on the grip is that you should keep the palms opposed. Bobby Locke, the South African, the best putter I ever saw, used his normal everyday grip, save that he had both thumbs straight down the shaft. Most modern professionals use a 'reverse overlap' grip, rather a mouthful which means they have the left index finger 'outside' and riding over the fingers of the right hand. This firms up the left wrist.

Bernhard Langer often putts with his left hand below his right. Jack Nicklaus has his right hand noticeably 'behind' the shaft, and seems to do it all with a push of his right hand. Bobby Jones and Bobby Locke had

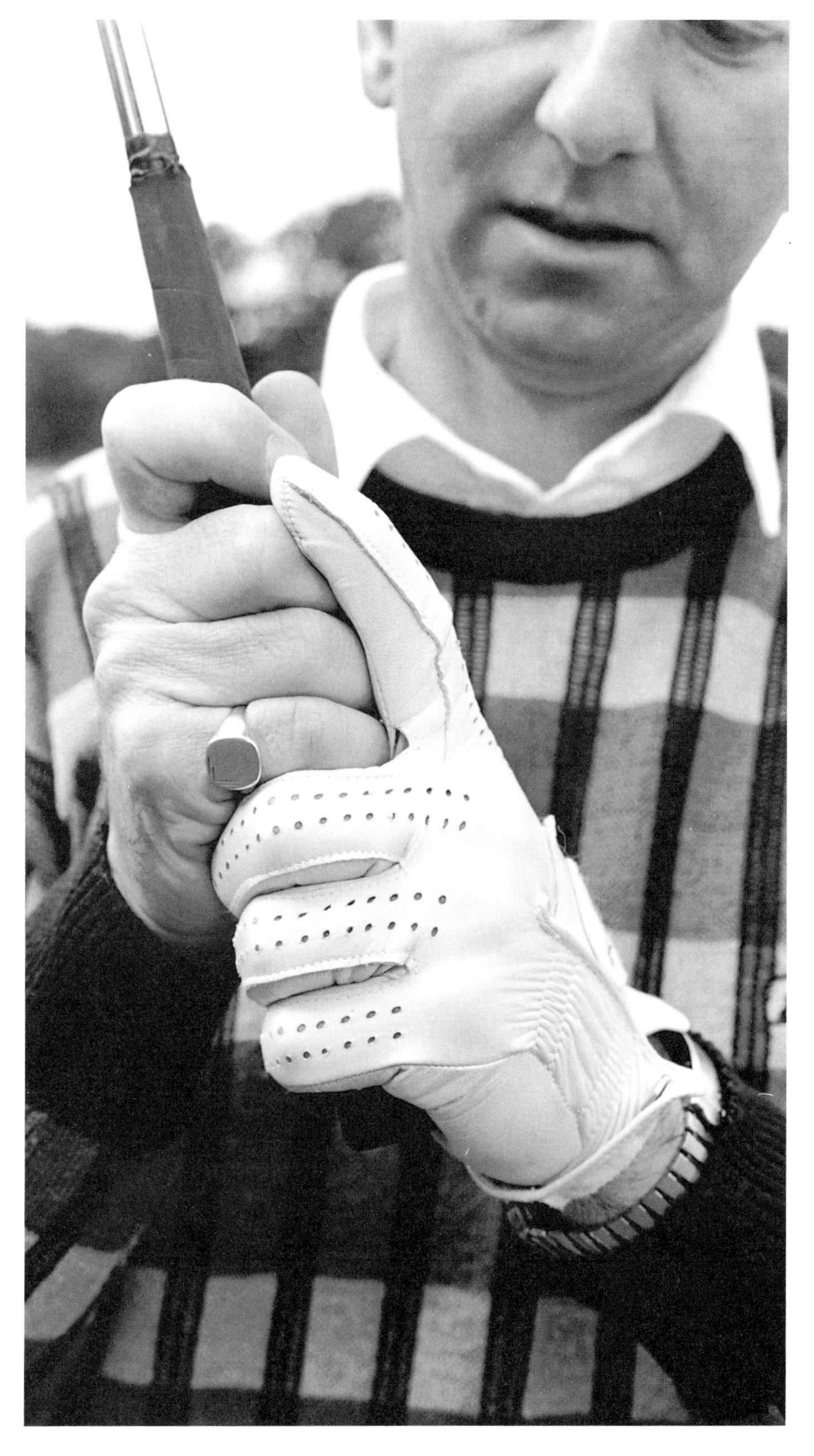

The reverse overlap grip as demonstrated by John Garner

their feet very close together in the stance, while Hubert Green, a US PGA champion, has a wide stance, weight all on the left foot, crouched over the ball, his hands in front of the ball and often separated on the shaft! Isao Aoki, the Japanese player, has the toe of the putter pointing in the air!

Bob Charles of New Zealand is a 'shoulder' putter. He keeps his wrists and arms stiff and uses a pendulum action from his shoulders. Billy Casper has more movement in his arms and wrists. All of these fellows have been or are fine putters but their variety of techniques proves only that there is no one way to do it. The best way is the way that works for you. If you are playing on slow, damp winter greens, you might think of using a putter fairly heavy in the head. If you are on quick, dry summer greens, you might well try a lighter head.

You must relax on the short putts. Above all, on the greens, you must be positive in everything you do. Putting is about confidence, or put more crudely, guts.

Chipping and Pitching

Golf, as you may have noted, is a strange game full of paradoxes. One of them is that the best of golfers, the great champions who are highly skilled in every aspect of the game, don't always reach the green in regulation figures on every hole that they play. Don't ask me why. I don't know, except that perhaps it is simply because they are human beings.

Consequently, we are faced with a whole department of golf in which we are required to play mini-shots, from relatively short distances, for various reasons. These are mainly because with the shot to the green, we have 'under-clubbed' and left the ball short of the target, or 'over-clubbed' and hit the ball too far, sending it skipping beyond the putting surface. Perhaps our direction is out – the ball has flown the correct distance, but is off-line and finishes to the left or right of the green, too often in a bunker placed to snare just such a shot. Or perhaps the gods of golf have frowned and put a stone where it should not have been, so that the simple bounce on towards the pin becomes a squirt off in the wrong direction.

Now we have to chip or pitch the ball up to the hole. It is as well to know the difference between these two shots. A chip shot is one in which we want minimum flight and maximum roll along the ground. A pitch shot is one in which we want maximum flight and minimum roll along the ground.

We chip the ball when it is just a few feet off the putting surface, or if the ground between the ball and the hole is relatively flat or without too many humps and hollows, no hazards, between ball and flagstick.

We pitch the ball when we want it to fly over rough or a hazard – bunker or stream – between ball and flagstick, or even when we are playing a full approach shot to the green from, say, around 100 yards, with a pitching wedge or a 9-iron.

Thus the chip shot is one in which we want to clip the ball on to the putting surface and have it *run* at the hole, and the pitch shot is one in

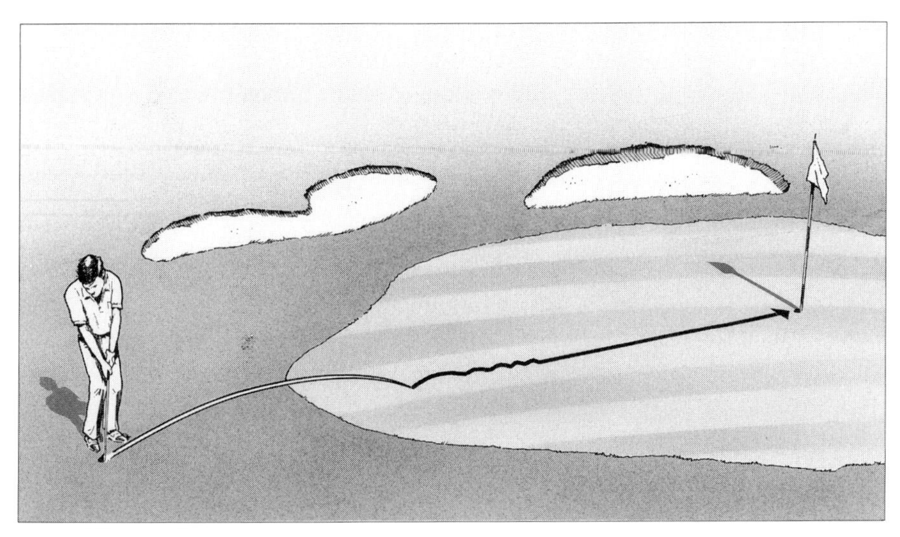

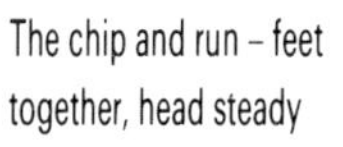

The chip and run – feet together, head steady

which we want to float the ball well on to the putting surface and have it stop near the flagstick after only a few yards of run.

The chip shot, played from a few feet from the edge of the putting surface, is an extension of the putt. You are rolling the ball towards the hole, letting it drop only just on the putting surface and running on to the hole, so that, just as in a putt, you are concerned with *line* and *speed*. Club selection can vary. If you are a few inches off the putting surface, you might use a 5-iron. If you are several feet away, you might use an 8-iron. Many golfers use the same club, say a 7-iron, for all chip shots – and perhaps that is sound technique for the average club golfer. One thing less to think about! You certainly want a club that will land the ball on the spot you have already chosen from which the ball will run to the hole.

You can even use a putter from off the putting surface, but make sure that the ground between you and the green is true and even, and that the grain of the grass is running with you and not against you. In all of these shots, however, you must have a clear picture in your mind as to the spot on which you want the ball to land and how it will behave from that spot.

The mechanics of the chip shot are simple. You need not concern yourself with body action – this is an arms and hands and clubhead shot. In playing it go through the same preliminaries as with any other golf shot. Set up the clubface square to the target line you have chosen. Take a correct grip of the club. Since it is a 'little' shot, your feet will be closer together, legs nicely flexed, in an altogether comfortable position. You should set your weight more on the left leg, with your hands slightly ahead of the ball position.

Don't crowd the ball, don't stand too close to it – you might withdraw your left foot an inch or two to help you swing through the ball, but you must keep your shoulders square to the target line. If you don't, you'll probably haul the ball to the left of the line.

All that is needed now is a smooth back and through swing, like a putt, accelerating through the ball with hands, arms and clubhead and almost no hinging of the wrists. If I am close to the edge of the putting

Pitching requires a full backswing especially when playing over a hazard

Pitching requires a good follow-through

surface and if the pin is on the far side of the green I use what I call a 'running' club, a 3, 4 or 5-iron. If the pin is close to my side of the green, I use what I call a 'flopping' club, an 8 or 9-iron or even a pitching wedge, with the blade slightly open. This will cut the ball up so that it flops on to the putting surface with a restricted run.

The pitch shot, short or long, is in turn an extension of the chip shot. The one important difference is that with the chip shot you are minimising backspin to allow the ball to run, and with the pitch shot, you are maximising backspin, to make it stop. The big difference in the mechanics of the shot is that in the pitch the wrists will hinge or cock on the backswing, uncock on the downswing. To get some backspin on the ball which makes it stop more quickly on the green, we have to strike the back of the ball with a rather steep, downward blow.

The preparation is unchanged – grip correct, blade square to the target line, stance more or less the same as for the chip, shoulders parallel to the line. The longer the shot, of course, the wider will be the stance. As in the chip shot, you can withdraw your left foot slightly to give the arms room to swing through. But *don't* open those shoulders!

Take the clubhead away smoothly, cock the wrists fairly early on the backswing, keep them cocked at the start of the downswing then release them with a smooth acceleration through the ball, with the hands ahead of the clubhead until after impact and with the head still. The one thing you do not want to do with this shot is hurry. Make it slow and smooth.

The distance you want to pitch the ball is governed by the length of your backswing. Some very good players have fixed three or four backswing positions in their minds for distance, so that if they want to pitch the ball 20–30 yards say, they swing to their 'Position A' at the top; for 30–50 yards they'll swing further back to 'Position B', 50–70 yards to 'Position C' and so on. If this works for you, use it! It will take practice.

Of course, if you are around 90 yards from the green, you will be playing a full pitch, with a 9-iron or pitching wedge, and a full backswing when your hands will be up around shoulder level with more upper body turn. With this shot you should shoot for the top of the flagstick – most of the trouble around greens is at the front or sides.

There are quite a few 'don'ts' in chipping and putting. In talking about golf, I prefer to talk about 'dos' rather than 'don'ts' – positive rather than negative. But in chipping and putting all the mistakes and mishits arise when we have failed to apply the fundamentals. These remain – keep the head still; swing the clubhead; accelerate the clubhead through the ball; keep the hands ahead of the ball until after impact. If you do that and forget about trying to scoop or squirt or stab or flick the ball forward, then your only concern will be line and speed.

Work hard on your chipping and putting practice. Think about these shots – getting them right can knock half a dozen strokes off your score.

Dr Golf himself – John Jacobs demonstrating at one of his world-famous clinics.

The masterclass in action: Peter Alliss, assisted by John Garner, coaches the television pupils at Letham Grange Golf and Country Club near Arbroath.

The 1-iron expert: Sandy Lyle at St Andrews.

Nick Faldo – the classic driving posture.

The Mexican Magician: The fairway iron shot as played by Lee Trevino.

Greg Norman smashing a long fairway iron at the 1986 US Masters, Augusta.

The world's most famous bunker player, 'The more practise, the luckier I get' Gary Player).

Laura Davies coming out of a bunker at the 1987 British Ladies' Open, St Mellion, Cornwall.

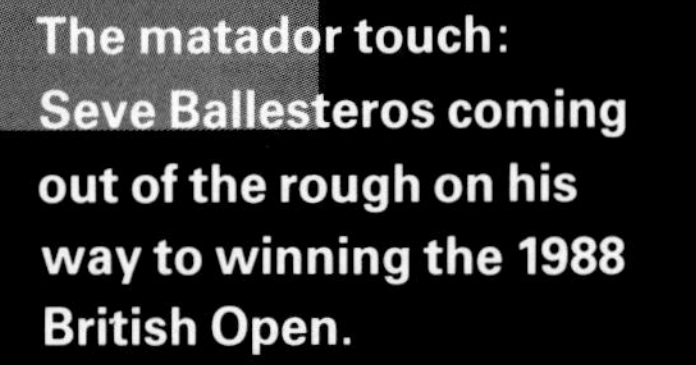

The matador touch: Seve Ballesteros coming out of the rough on his way to winning the 1988 British Open.

Coming out of the sand: Ian Woosnam on his way to winning the 1988 European Open at Sunningdale.

America's No 1 player Curtis Strange playing a metal wood.

Amy Alcott, putting on her way to winning the 1985 World Championship of Women's Golf.

Mark NcNulty's putting grip – note the position of the right finger.

Hubert Green's unique putting grip, stroke and stance.

The Great Bear's interlocking grip: Jack Nicklaus at St Andrews.

Bernhard Langer's renowned putting technique – the reverse overlap grip.

THE SAND

The best golfers in the world – Ballesteros, Lyle, Norman, Strange – find themselves in bunkers. They don't, after all, hit every drive, every approach shot, perfectly. Sometimes their perfectly good shots will bounce unpredictably and skip into the sand. This annoys them, but it doesn't worry them. They are not afraid of the sand – they know the shots that will get them out of there comfortably, because they have spent many hours practising these shots. In other words, they are disciples of the gospel according to Gary Player.

The major problem to be overcome by less-than-perfect golfers in these hazards is, as ever, fear, fear over what they believe are the most difficult situations, the most difficult shots, in golf. The bunker shot is not the most difficult shot in golf. All right it isn't the easiest, it's not as easy as a three-inch putt. But it isn't the most difficult if we know what is involved and face up to it. Dispelling fear is the first necessity and we can only do that if we have a clear idea of the problem and how to resolve it.

The problem is essentially the difference between turf and sand. Almost all orthodox golf shots, certainly all fairway shots, are played with the clubface striking the ball on a slightly downward path. The ball is then squeezed briefly between the clubface and the resistance of the turf and, as the turf gradually yields, the clubhead goes on through and up, the loft on the face of the club – 3-iron, 3-wood, 5-iron, 9-iron – thrusting the ball forwards and upwards into a natural trajectory.

Sand is not turf. Sand does not resist so that, if the ball is struck in the same way, it will simply be driven downwards and deeper into the sand and we will lose all control of it.

The most common bunker situation is by the green, in a bunker which has a raised front or lip so that we have to get the ball up to clear that lip and send it forward towards the hole. To do this we must make the clubface cut under the ball with a slicing action. In extracting the ball successfully, in popping it up and forward, we must also extract some sand. To do this, we need a specialised club, the sand wedge, and a specialised swing, one that is quite different from the orthodox golf swing.

The first thing to appreciate in this shot is that the clubface *never* contacts the ball. We strike the sand *behind* the ball and, appropriately enough, set up a 'sandwich' situation with sand as the filling between

Notice the steep, full backswing necessary when faced with a ball buried in a bunker

clubface and ball. Both sand and ball are splashed out of the bunker on to the putting surface. The distance we hit behind the ball and the strength of the blow will govern the length of the shot. I can't teach you this. No one can. You learn by experience, by play and practice.

The specialised sand wedge has a heavy rounded flange protruding in front of the leading edge of the club. This allows the clubhead to skid under the ball, splashing it and the sand up and out. You need a well-rounded flange in playing from very fine, soft sand, a less well-rounded flange from harder, more compacted sand. Check the type of sand common to your course and check with your professional that you have the correct sand wedge.

As I said, you need a specialist swing for this shot. It is probably the only shot in the game which you play with shoulders open to the target line. Make sure your set-up is right. Take a normal grip, position the ball opposite your left foot with feet and shoulders, your entire left side open, to the left of the target line. Open the clubface – the more open it is, the higher will be the flight of the ball. Then swing the clubhead *out to in*, with a swing path which goes *across* and *under* the ball and *across* the target line. In this shot you are swinging along the line of your shoulders and not along the target line. That open clubface will keep the ball on the target line.

Although there will be a substantial explosion of sand with the shot, you are not making a blast, you are making a splash. You will not make much of a deliberate shoulder turn on the shot, but you must make sure to turn your hips on the downswing, get them out of the way as it were, so that the clubface will stay open.

The most common mistake golfers make with bunker shots is to try to flick the ball out of the sand, usually with a short and frantic backswing, then some kind of spooning action on the ball. It doesn't work.

What you want is a smooth, unhurried backswing and the rhythmic action of a pitch shot, with a firm impact under and beyond the ball. Another fault is quitting on the shot at impact, letting the clubhead stop as it enters the sand. This is fatal. You must let the clubhead swing down, under and beyond the ball, and go on to a sensible follow-through, keeping the head still.

There is a modified version of this sand shot for the ball that is plugged in the sand, or almost buried in the bunker. You will have to 'dig' this one out. The procedure here is that you will use a steep swing and a sharp downward attack on the ball. Keep the hands ahead of the clubhead throughout the action. You will have the same grip, stance and ball position, but have the clubface closed. You break the wrists fairly early on the backswing and come down into the sand behind the ball with a healthy punch, down and through. The ball will be 'chopped' out of the sand. On this shot the ball will run a good deal further than from the splash shot and you will not have quite the same control over distance. But from that type of lie, getting out is the priority.

The fairway bunker shot poses different problems with different sol-

Opposite: the buried bunker shot – hitting down and through

Left: buried bunker shot follow-through should be restricted

For a greenside bunker shot aim about an inch or two behind the ball

utions. In the 1983 Ryder Cup matches in Florida, Ballesteros hit a 3-wood shot from a fairway bunker to the green – 245 yards away! All that we need to say about that is the man is a genius, then move on smartly to more mortal things.

The first requirement in tackling fairway bunker shots is to check the lie. If the ball is plugged, however slightly, if the lie is anything less than clear and clean and perfect, forget any fancy notions about distance. Just get it out.

The second thought in tackling a fairway bunker shot is to think of advancing the ball as far down the fairway as we can. The first obstacle is the height of the bank of the bunker between the ball and the target. So start your procedure from the side. Have a look at the height of the bank and decide on a club that will give you enough loft to clear that bank. Don't be greedy about this – if in any doubt, take more loft.

From here, we play a normal golf shot with the club we have selected. In other words, this time we contact ball before sand with a normal swing. If you ground the club in the hazard, in other words touch the sand with the club as you take up an address position, you are penalised! This can work for you as, by keeping the clubhead just clear of the sand at address, it will help you take up a correct stance and give you the impression that you are really in control of the club.

It is important to remain centred on these shots, with no body sway and with head still. To help with this you should try to keep more of your weight on your left side throughout the swinging action, keep the hands ahead of the clubhead into the ball and hit through solidly into a balanced follow-through. One danger is in over-swinging and falling about. Shorten your backswing. Balance throughout the action is probably the most important single factor in this shot.

Don't forget to take a full backswing on all bunker shots

Hit through the ball on bunker shots

The ordinary bunker shot demands a full follow-through

There is less to fear from sand shots than you may think. Before you even step into the hazard, the bunker, take an overall look at the situation. Look at the lie, the quality of the sand, the height of the front of the bunker, how the whole thing relates to your target. Have a clear idea of what you want to achieve as you step into the bunker and play the shot confidently and positively.

Take a few practice swings outside the bunker. Don't just swing the club, practise the kind of swing and stance you are going to use when you do step into the bunker. I can promise you that an hour or two of practice will work wonders for your bunker play. It will give you a confidence in yourself which will spread through the rest of your game.

LIES, AND DAMNED LIES

A golf course, alas, is not a snooker table. Fairways rise and fall and tumble in all directions so that we often have to play uphill, downhill, sidehill shots, especially on seaside courses.

The first general thought you should have in tackling such lies is that you have to relate your stance and body position to the plane of the slope by staying perpendicular to that slope. Your swing in these shots will depend on your stance even more than it does on all the other shots. You must have a clear idea of how to control your upper body weight in these shots and, just as important, a clear idea of how the clubface should be moving through the ball.

On an uphill lie, for instance, if you stand perpendicular to the slope, your right shoulder will be lower than normal and your weight will tend to be on the downhill side, the right side. It should be easier to start a low backswing from this attitude. Do that. Your follow-through, following the plane of the upslope, should come up rather more quickly than usual.

Since most of your weight will be inclined to stay on your right side, it will be easy to hook the ball. Aim slightly to the right of your target. Since you are hitting uphill, the ball will fly higher than usual and cover less distance. You may want to take more club than usual. What you want to avoid in this shot is driving the club into the ground *after* impact with the ball.

A downhill lie is the other side of the same coin. The downslope will tend to push most of your weight on to the downside, the left side, but again you must try to stay perpendicular to the slope with your stance. The slope will force you to pick up the clubhead quite early on the backswing, and you must concentrate on hitting *down* the slope, with the clubhead going *down* and *through* the ball, following the ball exactly down the plane of the slope. Don't try to get the ball into the air – let the loft on the clubface do that for you.

Since most of your weight will be inclined to stay on your left side, it will be easy to slice the ball. Aim slightly to the left of your target. You are hitting downhill so the ball will fly lower than normal and further. You may want to take less club than usual. What you want to avoid in this shot is driving the clubhead into the ground *before* impact with the ball.

Opposite
Top left: for the downhill lie – aim slightly left of target

Top right: the downhill lie – keep more weight on your right side

Bottom left: hit down and through the slope

Bottom right: the downhill lie – note the restricted follow-through

The influence of these slopes on weight transference in the golf swing is the problem. You should cut down your upper body movement. Don't be greedy about distance. Staying in balance throughout the swinging action is very important and you will find it a help to have rather more weight forward, towards your toes, in the stance.

Apart from practice on the practice ground, which will do wonders for your confidence in coming to terms with these shots, when you are on the golf course, I recommend practice swings – half a dozen, if you like. These will give you the feel of the action, of staying in balance, of how the clubface should be contacting the ball, of how the clubhead should be parallel to the ground in those few inches before, at and after contact.

On downhill lies you should have the feeling that you are staying 'at the back of the ball' and are giving a good solid smack to the back of the ball. On uphill lies you should feel that you are 'in front of the ball', certainly with your hands, and that you are not going to fall back and scoop the ball into the air.

If the ball is above your feet you will have to stand more upright than usual and take a stance a little further from the ball. This will make you swing in a rather flatter plane and tend to hook the ball, so I would grip down the shaft slightly and aim off to the right, simply allowing the ball to hook. You should content yourself with a three-quarter swing – again, stay in balance.

If the ball is below your feet it will be further away than in a normal, flat lie. You will have to bend over to reach it so you should stand closer to it, with the legs perhaps more flexed at the knee than in a normal stance. Your swing will be more upright than normal so grip at the end of the shaft and aim off, this time to the left, since the ball will likely slice a little. You don't want too much body movement, as in all these 'unusual' shots, so concentrate on making it arms, hands and clubhead action, and again – stay in balance.

Take several practice swings to get the feel of your relationship to the slope and, as in all these shots, keep your head still.

One of the most infuriating happenings in this game comes when you have hit a perfectly good shot down the fairway and arrive at the ball to find it nestling neatly in a divot mark, someone else's divot mark. There it is – a perfectly good fairway offering excellent lies, only an inch or two away on either side. It means that someone who passed this way ahead of you was guilty of impoliteness, of ungentlemanly conduct, was not, in short, a true golfer. But there it is – you must make the best of it.

You should think of playing a regulation shot – don't overestimate the challenge of divot shots – but with a firmer, crisper action. Keep the hands slightly forward, keep more of the weight on the left side and have the feeling that you are hitting down and through the ball more firmly than you would from a fairway lie.

One of the best thoughts you can have with these divot shots, in getting through the ball and moving it forward and upward out of that hole, is *extend the divot*. Making the divot longer, stretching out in the direction

Playing out of a divot – hands and weight forward, hit down and follow through

of the hole, will help you make a very positive strike at the ball and will demand a full follow-through.

If you are caught in a divot mark near the green, don't use a pitching wedge. The sharper edge of an 8-iron or 9-iron will give you better control on these shorter shots.

BUBBLE, BUBBLE, TOIL AND TROUBLE

Much of the anguish of golf comes from hitting into trouble, hitting the ball into rough ground or difficult places. Every course has them, every golfer in his time visits a variety of them, every golfer has to deal with them, one way or the other. But equally, a good deal of the delight in the game lies in getting out of these places, in getting out of trouble.

On the average course, there is a splendid variety of the stuff in store for the innocent, unsuspecting player – long grass, heather and bracken, trees, water, bare lies, even divot marks in the middle of the fairway. And when a golfer hits into trouble, he automatically hits into a splendid variety of emotional trouble!

He is probably furiously angry with himself for having done it, for having hooked or sliced or skulled the ball into such places. So, as he strides after the ball, he is probably in a good deal of unhealthy emotional turmoil. Or, perhaps he is furiously angry with the unknown gods of the game who have caused his ball to bounce erratically in there. Oh, it isn't fair, it isn't fair! Also crowding into his mind is the thought that he will have to redeem this by making his next shot exceptional, by playing a super-shot, a perfect shot, a miracle shot.

This is aggression. The golfer would do well to forget it, to put all that out of his mind, for this is a time for having intelligence in control. He must accept that 'he put it there'. It is up to him to get it out of there. So the first rule is to calm down. It is a time to accentuate the positive, eliminate the negative and, above all, cultivate the 'art of the possible'.

There are two basics in these situations. The first is *get it out*! The second is *advance the ball*, if you can!

The obvious object of the exercise is to get the ball into a playable lie, that is, back on the fairway. This should be the overwhelming ambition. If you can do that, then to advance the ball even 20 or 30 yards nearer the hole – on the fairway – should be the supplementary ambition.

The first step is to have your emotions under control. The next is to engage the gears of the mind and survey the scene. Look at the lie of the ball – is it nestling down in deep grass, for instance? Can you take a reasonable stance to the ball and be able to set the clubhead correctly behind it? Then check an imaginary swing – will you be able to make a complete backswing and follow-through?

At one end of the scale of escape is a ball lying lightly in two or three inches of rough grass not far off the fairway. If that is so, you can get to the ball and play a perfectly orthodox golf shot. At the other end of the scale is the ball that plopped into the middle of a lake or is underneath a huge rhododendron bush. That makes life easy! You don't have to be in the decision business now. You are unplayable and are obliged to drop another ball under penalty, as prescribed by the rules, and play on.

Between these extremes is a range of situations which will demand that you make decisions. You must always remember that in these recovery shots, the key word is 'recovery'. That is the priority. If you find that you cannot make a proper swing at, and contact with, the ball – there may be overhanging branches or the ball may be in tree roots – cut your losses and drop out according to the rules. Take the prescribed penalty. It will save you shots in the long run.

If you can make a passable contact with the ball you must then consider

(a) your escape route

(b) how to fashion in your mind the shot and the contact between clubface and ball and

(c) club selection.

When top professionals are in a trouble spot, you may think they spend a long time prowling around the situation, marching forward, marching back, picking away from the ball little leaves you'd think would make not the slightest difference to the shot. They are not wasting time. They are considering all the options – what kind of stroke they want to use, how the ball will behave, where it will go? You must do likewise.

The escape route has to be established. If the way is 'open' between the ball and your target point, whether it is the green or a spot on the fairway, with no hazards or trees intervening, fine. Go ahead and play the orthodox shot. In fashioning this shot, you must remember that grass will be sandwiched between the clubface and the ball. This reduces the friction created between the grooves on the club and the ball and therefore reduces the backspin applied to the ball, which will tend to fly lower and run further on landing. The more grass that comes between clubface and ball, the less effective the shot will be. Sometimes really heavy stuff twists the shaft slightly so that the hit becomes less than pure.

The tendency for the ball to scoot and run on these shots is what the professionals call 'a flier'. This simply means that the ball will fly off the clubface, giving them less control over distance than they would have on a similar shot played from the fairway. So you might be wise to take one club less and allow for the extra run.

If you are in heavy rough, with the ball deep in the grass, you will have to modify your action. You have to hit this one smartly and powerfully. You pick the club up more quickly by breaking the wrists early in the backswing, and get down into the ball with a solid punch. This is absolutely necessary if you are in heather – it is foul stuff and needs a solid smash and a follow-through to get the ball away.

Trees

Trees abound on most British golf courses, the links courses excepted. I have always been very suspicious of trees on golf courses and have a healthy regard for them. They are best avoided – trees are by no means the golfer's friend.

If you are in the rough and are faced with trees between you and your target, there are clear alternatives. You can go over them, round them, through them, under them. You could also outflank them by ignoring them, by simply knocking your ball out to the side, to the fairway, and so removing this obstruction from your path. That is not the coward's way – it will have cost you one stroke, but rattling around in the trees can cost you any number of strokes.

I am constantly astonished by the way the average golfer tries to cope with trees and by the impossible shots he uses to solve the problem. No doubt these are throwbacks to his notion that after a sloppy shot which put him in the rough, why, he'll just produce a miracle shot to cancel that out. It's not on. It doesn't work. The odds are solidly against you.

If you decide to go over the trees, you need a club with the loft to clear the highest tops and at the same time give you the length to carry the depth of the wood. Hmmm.

If you decide to go round them, that means you have enough confidence to draw or fade the ball round one end of the trees or the other – from a lie in the rough? Hmmm.

If you decide to go 'through' them, stop right there. I am astonished at the number of average golfers, very average golfers, I see blasting away at a gap in the trees of no more than three feet in the sublime hope that they can do what Señor Ballesteros could not do – and wouldn't even attempt to do! The result is a great clattering of golf balls and branches, of falling leaves and the case of the vanishing golf ball. True, it may rebound to the fairway – it might. But most of the time it means a lost ball, or a place that is worse, and deeper in the woods, and more and more strokes gone. Consider the odds – don't do it!

If you are under a tree and the branches are such as to allow you a proper swing, and the lie is reasonable, go ahead and swing – don't let the tree inhibit you. But if the tree or trees are in front of you and you have to play a low shot under branches, you have a little more thinking to do. To keep the ball low select a more straight-faced club, virtually a long iron, play the ball back towards your right foot with the face closed a little, keep your hands in front of the ball, and give it a good punch. If you play this shot correctly the ball will stay low and run a good distance. Include that extra run in your calculations.

The Rough

Often you will find a ball 'sitting up' in the rough, an inch or two from the ground, usually where the grass is not overlong. This gives you the chance to 'sweep' the ball away, rather than 'smash' it away. The trick is not to ground the club at address but to set the clubface exactly behind

Playing a 5-wood from semi-rough

the ball, off the ground. The important thing in this shot is to look at the ball, to stay in balance during the swing and, I'd say, take a three-quarter swing.

In tackling trouble spots, and there is an abundance of them, major and minor, on any golf course, you have to use your imagination. You'd be surprised what a putter can do for you, particularly from a bare lie or even light rough. A good knock with a putter can advance the ball 30 or 40 yards which, depending on the terrain and the conditions, may be just what you want.

You can use the putter from very light rough, just off the fairway, with the same effect. You would be well advised to use the putter from bare lies just off the green – from a path, for instance – in what would otherwise be a chip shot. A lofted club used from such a lie is certainly not recommended.

Sometimes, I hope not often, you can find a lie in which the ball is hard by a tree or a wall or some other obstruction where you cannot take a normal stance. Simply stand on the 'other' side of the ball, with your back to the hole or the target, and give it a whack, one-handed. Use a 7, 8, or 9-iron, which have larger heads and position the clubhead behind the ball with the toe pointing down. You could even try a left-handed swing at the ball, with left hand below right and the clubhead reversed and pointed down, but I must say at the risk of boring you that these shots need some practice.

Wind

Playing in strong winds can be a real test of your mental health. Be rational about it. If the wind is against you, the ball will not fly so far. If the wind is with you, the ball will fly further. Obvious? Trite? Certainly – but accept the facts. Don't fight the wind. You cannot win. So make it an ally.

If the wind is strong enough, of course, it could affect your stance and your swinging action. Unless you are playing in a gale, which we can all do without, you can adjust to this by taking a slightly narrower stance, reducing your swing length and body action and making a positive effort to stay in balance. This should make a good, square contact with the ball. The word here is to keep everything compact.

Playing against the wind, you should accept that all that is happening is that the wind is making the hole a little longer, perhaps turning a par four into a par five. So, play it as a par five. Your instinct will be to hit the ball harder, to have a real smash at it. Resist this instinct. Again, keep everything more compact. Grip the club slightly down the shaft, and try to keep the hands leading the clubhead right through. For shots to the green take more club – which is another way of saying use your common sense and imagination.

Playing downwind, you will appreciate that the hole is being made a little shorter. Perhaps a 3-wood from the tee will give you better control than a driver. On shots to the green you will have less than your usual control – the ball will tend to sprint away from you on landing – so take a club or two less. The temptation with downwind shots is to be greedy

Opposite: Pip Elson demonstrating the dreaded shank

Top right: rolling the clubface open on the backswing

Bottom left: hands too far ahead of the club on the downswing

Bottom right: result – ball hit off the shank of the club

and give them some extra muscle and hit the ball out of sight. Not necessary as the wind will do all that for you. You might think of teeing the ball slightly forward to help you elevate the ball but again you must use a controlled swing. The wind tends to reduce the backspin on these shots which makes the flight lower and makes the ball run further on landing.

The most important factor in all wind shots is control. If the wind is crossing you right to left, aim off to the right. If it is crossing you from the left, aim off to the left. Let the wind carry the ball back into the fairway. Simple, obvious, but control is the thing – keep the ball in play, on the fairway.

Rain

The same is true when playing in the rain on a wet course. In the rain you must keep the grips dry and your hands dry but a towel which can be stowed in the bag will take care of that. If you wear a glove and it gets too wet for comfort, is no longer doing its job, change it or abandon it. We all have to make sacrifices!

The main technical challenges on wet weather play are to make clean and square contacts with all shots. Let's face it, it is quite difficult to hit fairway wood shots and long iron shots from soggy fairways. Sacrifice distance in return for correct contact with the ball and take 'shorter' clubs and use 'quieter' swings.

So, to sum up recovery from the rough places which you are likely to encounter in any round of golf:

1 Think – stay cool, my friend, and get your emotions under control. Don't just hit and hope.
2 Get out.
3 Advance the ball, if you can.
4 Don't go for the possible shot. Don't go for the probable shot. Go for the likely shot or, better still, the certain shot, the one that will certainly get you out of trouble, and
5 Relish the tough spots – they are part of the rich tapestry of the game. Meet their challenge!

Finally, there is one other area of trouble in this game, perhaps the most important of all. That is, when we get into trouble with ourselves, with our swing, when something goes wrong with it. When it does, it is our own fault. There is no one else to blame in golf!

The first thing to do when your swing is not behaving itself is to sit down and think about it. The second thing is to beware of rushing to the practice ground. Too often that is where we practise our faults. When Peter Thomson, the great Australian champion, had something not quite right in his swing he didn't rush to the practice ground. He would go back to his hotel, sit quietly on his own for half an hour or so and analyse in his mind what he had been doing. Then he'd say, 'That's it – I've got it!' and only then would he go to the practice ground and hit a few shots.

4
B51
XTC

The treatment for a faulty golf swing is rather like the procedure for any ailment. You start with analysis, or diagnosis. If it is a minor fault such as lifting the head, quitting on bunker shots, getting your feet positions wrong in the stance, then a little thought and a session on the practice ground can put it right.

This is the aspirin treatment – if you have a slight headache, you take care of it yourself without rushing to the doctor. But if the ailment is chronic, potentially terminal – persistent slicing, shanking, topping – then it is time for the doctor, the specialist, the consultant. In golf, that means the professional. He'll be able to tell exactly what is wrong at a glance, or at least after you have hit three or four shots, and he will put it right very quickly. And the few pounds he charges you will be money well spent, cheap at the price.

Our times and the world being what they are, if anyone decides to take up golf now and equip himself for the game on a grand scale he can probably spend a thousand pounds without trying too hard. He might be indulging his ego, flaunting his lifestyle or causing a minor flutter in the cash flow, but this kind of thing would simply not be necessary.

Over the past 20 years golf, international golf in particular, has had so much television exposure and has grown so much world-wide, that the marketing of clubs and balls and clothing now represents a huge industry. There are dozens and dozens of club manufacturing companies, many of them Japanese. In terms of clothing, the 'rag trade' has completely changed the golfer's attitude to his appearance. The old gardening trousers, the old brogues, nowadays simply will not do – now golfers wear 'customised matching outfits' from top to toe and I think the game is all the better for it.

But to the innocent abroad the promotional language manufacturers use as selling points can be bewildering. He is overwhelmed by cavity-backed irons, radial soles, peripheral weightings, off-set and anti-shank irons, hollow irons, tumble finish, ceramic plastic-coated irons, graphite shafts, titanium shafts, carbon fibre this, beryllium copper that, not to mention four-way radius contoured soles!

My advice to the absolute beginner is to ignore all this. Second-hand clubs are the thing for you. Find yourself half a dozen of them – the professional at your local club will probably have a barrelful of oddments. Use these clubs until you get some notion of the golf swing, of how to stand to the ball, of the sensation of the clubhead making a reasonable contact with the ball. Then, when you are hooked on the game and want to play more correctly, more seriously, more regularly, think of buying some new clubs.

Begin with a half set of a couple of wooden clubs, half a dozen irons and a putter. A good putter with which you are comfortable is critically important – it should be your best friend in the game! Until you find more confidence in your game, the 3-wood will give you more loft from the tee than will a driver and you'll find it easier to get the ball into the air. You'll use the other wooden club, probably a 5-wood, for the longer fairway shots.

At this point, you must invest in some advice from a professional. The important things that he will establish about your new clubs are that the length and stiffness of the shafts, the weight of the clubs and the lie of the clubs – the angle made between the shaft and the clubhead as it is set behind the ball – are absolutely right for you. In doing that, he will take into consideration your height, physique, age and the kind of swing you make at the ball.

A few years ago there was a short-lived fashion for shafts made of aluminium. Now, they are made of lightweight steel, or graphite, the advantage of graphite being that it is very light. However, graphite is liable to have more torque, that is it will twist more, and on the whole you might do better to stay with the traditional steel shaft. By all means try graphite and try too the 'metal woods' which have lighter heads than traditional woods. Your professional will have spares that I am sure he will let you try. Do accept his advice on all the equipment which is best for you. Tournament professionals play with very stiff shafts – they hit the ball very hard! You will be best suited by the 'R' shaft, the regulation shaft.

In the same way, tournament professionals play with balls of higher compression than the average. The compression of a ball, in simple terms, relates to the tightness of the winding of the rubber threads inside it. Modern golf balls come in two different types, the wound ball and the two-piece ball.

The wound ball has rubber thread wound tightly around a core that may be made of liquid, steel or paste. The whole thing is then wrapped in a cover. The two-piece ball does not have rubber threads but has a larger rubber core inside a cover. These covers are made of balata, a rubber substitute, or Surlyn, a synthetic material produced by the Du Pont Company in 1967. Surlyn is virtually indestructible, a great advantage to beginners, while balata gives perhaps more of that indefinable 'feel' that golfers experience at impact.

Advances in the manufacture of golf balls over the past 20 years have been so remarkable that modern balls are as uniform as they can possibly be and of a very high quality. But don't believe manufacturers when they say their ball flies further than the other fellows'. They don't. Machine tests in America have proved that the margin between different makes, different compressions, is seldom more than a few yards. I would say 100 compression is too hard for the average player – he should stick to not more than 90 compression in the ball of his choice.

For the rest, we are into fashion and whatever excites you in clothing – slacks, shirts, sweaters, hats, gloves and the like. You can manage very well with a lightweight bag, with compartments for balls, waterproof clothing and so on. You might want to use a pull-trolley, or even a powered trolley – there is ample choice. If you play in these British islands, you'd better have an umbrella.

In general, in golf as in everything else in life you should have the very best equipment your budget will allow. Now that you have the tools, you can get on with the job!

PRACTICE WITH A PURPOSE

In the good old days, if there ever were such days, there was an attitude throughout British sport that the game was the thing, the *playing* of the game, and that practice was somehow something which a 'gentleman' simply did not do. It was a philosophy which happily is all but dead in every sport, from archery to wrestling.

In golf as in almost all human activity, the more you practise, the better you will become, provided you practise with a purpose. In golf, practice is just as important, just as critical to the making of a golfer, as is the game itself. If you are taking the game seriously you want to be as good as you can be. You want to maximise your potential. But since there are other things in life, other claims on your time, you have to decide what sacrifices you are prepared to make, precisely how much time you can give to the game.

Regardless of your current standard of play don't discount the pleasures of the game or what you really can achieve. If the Open Championship is one end of the spectrum, your club's monthly medal may be the other and, with a sensible preparation, there is no reason why you should not win that medal. If you are 18 handicap and play at a course which has a par of 72, your personal par becomes 90. Scoring the course in 85 is not beyond you if you work at it – and your 85 is the exact equivalent of a 67 from the scratch player. But you will have to play well!

The purpose of practice is to create a repeating swing so that when you go on to the golf course you don't have to think too much about the swing, regardless of any minor imperfections it may have. Then you can concentrate your mind on scoring.

There are two types of practice. One is your work on the practice ground where you are laying the foundations of a swing, with all clubs. The other is what I could call 'warm-up' practice: the few practice shots or swings you would make before stepping on to the first tee. Don't let's start with a cold engine.

In going to the practice ground your first chore, yet again, is to think. You must think about what you did last time out, what you did that displeased you, why you are out there on the practice ground about to hit 20, 50 or 100 balls. You must never go to the practice ground without a definite idea on which you are going to work. It may be staying centred

'Can't I plead with you, Helen? It isn't my wish that our marriage should end like this'.

over the ball, slowing the backswing, tempo, or whatever. But you must have a very clear idea of what you are trying to achieve in the time, the valuable time, that you have. Make sure that the balls you use are clean and sound. A gashed ball will not fly truly and flight is an important clue as to what you are doing.

An excellent start to any practice session is to take a 7-iron and half a dozen balls and chip them out, some 25–30 yards. This will give you the feeling that your hands and arms are working; that your grip and stance are in place; that you can stay still over the shot but, more than anything else, it will remind you of the swinging clubhead, critical to all golf shots.

Most people work progressively through the bag, from pitching wedge to driver, and that is fine. I have often thought that fairly early in a practice session it can be valuable to hit a few 5-iron shots. These will give you the loft and distance to establish a flight pattern and, as we saw early in this book, the flight of the ball will always tell you what's right, or wrong, with the swing.

Between every shot you should step away, then once more take a correct grip of the club and come back to the next ball with a correct stance and concentrate on every single shot. You are not out there simply to blast dozens of balls into an empty field. You should hit to a specific target. If your practice ground doesn't have them, set them up yourself – an umbrella, a practice bag, anything.

If your practice isn't working, stop. Have a break. Think. Think of what you are doing wrong and how you can right it. There are times, of course, when the chemistry is wrong, when the liver or the mental process, is not at its best. Go away and come back another day.

But what you can do is handle a golf club every single day, if only for five minutes at a time. Just pick it up with a correct grip and make small swings, waggles if you like, which will strengthen the fingers, keep your grip in place and give you the feel of the wrists working, the clubhead swinging.

If you are not making a reasonably satisfactory swing, don't play. There is no point. You will never get any better on the course. The practice ground is where you must find the magic elixir of the sound swing. And I am not suggesting that your swing should be the Nick Faldo swing. When I say satisfactory swing, I mean one that will allow you to control the ball, put it where you want it to be on the fairway or on the green. If you fade the ball slightly, draw it slightly, so be it, as long as you have ball control.

If you have a garage you can rig up a net in it. You can chip in the garden, if you have a garden (from a piece of old carpet to protect the lawn). You can putt in the bedroom. You must give the game all the time you have allotted to it and on a regular basis. Then you'll be as good as you can be and a lot better than you ever thought you could be.

The other kind of practice, the mini-practice or warm-up, comes just before playing if you have not had time to spend on the practice ground. It is what it says it is: a means of warming the muscles, increasing the blood supply to them, reminding them of what they will have to do, 're-discovering' the swing, and establishing your 'thought for the day'.

Again, I would recommend that you pitch out half a dozen balls with, say, a 7-iron from the side of the tee into the rough along the edge of the fairway, 20 yards or so, to get the hands and arms working and the clubhead swinging.

And if your course does not have an established practice ground, don't make excuses or wallow in self-pity. Nag the committee, really agitate them, to make one. If there simply isn't enough available ground, nag them to set up nets near the first tee. Practising into a net is much better than not practising, not warming up, at all.

Finally, practice with a purpose can be a pleasure and it isn't necessarily purgatory. Your general overall thought in going to the practice ground is that this is the place where you prepare yourself to play better golf.

Finally, finally, finally, and by the way, do practise your putting. That may well be the most profitable practice of all.

PLAY THE GAME, SIR, PLAY THE GAME

> In golf, customs of etiquette and decorum are just as important as rules governing play. It is appropriate for spectators to applaud successful strokes in proportion to difficulty, but excessive demonstrations by a player or his partisans are not proper because of the possible effect on other competitors.
>
> Most distressing to those who love the game of golf is the applauding or cheerings of misplays or misfortunes of a player. Such occurrences have been rare at the Masters, but we must eliminate them entirely if our patrons are to continue to merit their reputations as the most knowledgeable and considerate in the world.

These words were written by Bobby Jones and first issued to the gallery, the 'patrons', at the US Masters of 1967 as they have been every year since. Golf is a gentleman's game and it should be played as gentlemen would play it. We are talking here about the etiquette of the game, which means no more than good manners, proper behaviour to a partner or opponent, and indeed to everyone on the course and in the clubhouse. We are talking about obeying both the letter and the spirit of the rules.

Jones was doing no more than echoing the part played by etiquette and good behaviour in the Rules of Golf rather than the rules of play, which are administered by the Royal and Ancient Golf Club of St Andrews and the United States Golf Association. There are 34 Rules of Golf with all kinds of subsections, appendices, definitions and decisions on strange incidents which have arisen on the course. But the very first section of the Rules concerns itself with 'Etiquette – Section One – Courtesy on the Course'. That is how important it is.

Unlike other sports, golf does not have a drugs or hooligan problem and there is no cheating in golf. However, there have been one or two disquieting signs lately – at the last two Ryder Cup matches and at recent Open Championships and other events – when crowd behaviour has not been as it should have been. There has been partisanship and screaming, shouting and whistling (why whistling, for heaven's sake?) around the last green at the Open which has gone far beyond enthusiastic applause.

One of the basic tenets of the game is that 'golfers don't cheat'. This is certainly not an absolute. Of course golfers cheat – they are human beings. But most often they cheat in the most trivial way, in the long run cheating themselves rather than the other man. No one can cheat the game itself. In general, the game is conducted by everyone obeying a sensible code.

So, Section One of the Rules is concerned with safety of play, consideration for others, priorities on the course and the repairing of damage to the course. We might take a look at the whole thing as we proceed from tee to green, as it were:

Get to the first tee ahead of your starting time. Don't be late. That is simple courtesy. If you are late, your match will hold up the entire starting sequence, you will miss your turn, or you'll be shunted to 'the back of the queue'. On a particularly busy day you might not be able to find another starting time!

Check the number of clubs in your bag – 14 is the current maximum allowed.

Check the golf balls being used in your group – if more than one of you is playing the same make and number, put a distinguishing mark on your ball.

If you want to make practice swings, do that off the tee, behind it.

Stand still when others are playing. The best position is by the tee box or marker facing the golfer in play. Then he knows exactly where you are.

Be quiet when others are playing.

You must tee your ball in the area, bounded by two club-lengths, behind a line between the markers, but not in front of that line. The ball must be inside that area – your stance may be outside it.

If you tee your ball in front of that line in stroke play you will have to replay the tee shot, incurring a two-stroke penalty. In match play you may be asked to replay the shot, without penalty.

If the ball falls off the tee peg as you prepare to play you may simply replace it, without penalty, provided you have not made a stroke at the ball.

If you start with less than 14 clubs you can add clubs during the round up to that limit. If you break a club in play, i.e. in playing a shot, you can replace it. If you snap one across your knee in a fit of pique or anger you cannot replace it. Such an action would be bad manners in any case.

Before driving off, make sure that the players ahead of you are out of range.

Down the fairway the same courtesies apply: don't stand too close to your partner or opponent when he is playing, stand still and stand quietly. Don't jingle coins or keys in your pocket and no sneezes, however inadvertent.

The Rules of Golf say 'In the interests of all, players should play without undue delay.' No one has been able to define 'undue delay' or just how long a round of golf should take. The weather, the difficulty of the course, the traffic on the course, whether you are playing a single, foursome or four-ball, will affect your pace. But it is reasonable to move along briskly between shots and give some thought to how you will play the next shot as you approach your ball before you even reach it. Everyone in your group should follow the flight of everyone else's shot – then if a ball goes into the rough, there is a better chance of it being found more quickly.

You are allowed to take five minutes in searching for a ball before deeming it 'lost'. If another match comes up behind you, you can't ask them to wait five minutes – let them play through. If the hole ahead of you is clear and people behind you are waiting, wave them through. When you have played your shot replace the divot or smooth out the sand.

The green is where play is more concentrated and where you can display your best manners. You can repair pitch marks on the green, made by the ball, but, under the present rules, you cannot repair heel marks, spike marks or any other marks on the green until after everyone has putted.

The player furthest from the pin will putt first. While he is doing that, you have the chance to study the line of your putt, have some idea of how you will play it and be ready when your turn comes.

You don't stand on the line of another golfer's putt. When marking your ball, you do it on the side away from the hole and check that your marker has left the other player's line clear. Try to stand outside of the line of vision of the golfer putting. Don't let anything, flagstick or golf clubs, drop on the green and when all the putting is finished make sure the flagstick is properly replaced. Then move smartly off the green if the match behind is waiting to play.

In this way, everyone is helping everyone else. Except in major tournaments and championships, there are no referees in golf. So the player's conscience is his own referee. It is all a matter of honour and trust. There are many situations in the game when it is easy to cheat – if a player is deep in woods, or out of sight of his opponents, or in replacing the ball on the green. Real golfers don't do these things, just as they don't shout or swear or throw clubs.

Courtesy is important when visiting other clubs. You should always write or telephone in advance and establish that you are welcome, confirming starting times, costs, etc. You should also check in advance the club's rules of dress, catering arrangements and so on. On arrival, pay your respects to the secretary or manager, pay green fees, collect cards and have a close look at the local rules before you tee off. You will be a member for the day – so you should behave as well as regular members are expected to do.

All of this is no more than common politeness. Golf is an honourable game. We should all try to keep it that way.

Somewhere along the long and winding road to perfection in this game, the novice golfer will make two startling discoveries – he does not live in a perfect world and there is more to golf than hitting the ball.

If we consider the perfect golf shot to be one in which the ball behaves exactly as, and finishes exactly where, the player intended, even the very greatest champions the game has known would all say that this happens no more than three or four times in any round. Nobody hits the ball correctly on every single shot. Even the marvellously low scores which the modern tournament professional is now producing, the 62s and 63s round big courses, will provoke the comment 'It could have been better, if only. . . .'

Perhaps that is simply saying that the golfer is never satisfied. But in thinking of this game in a more general, even philosophical, way there comes a time when we have to be satisfied. This chapter is essentially about just that – how we should be thinking about the game, about scoring the course.

Under certain conditions, Sandy Lyle can hit the ball 300 yards with a 1-iron! But then Lyle is a young man, a golfer of great strength and talent, at the peak of his career. A man of, say 50, does not have the physical power or energy of a man of 25 years. This is why you must *know* what you can achieve, and attempt *only* what you can achieve.

It has been said that good golf is a 'state of mind' and this is substantially true. It is a tantalising and maddening game, demanding at the same time concentration and relaxation, and its inherent unfairness – the difficulty of striking the ball consistently correctly, the unpredictable bounce of the ball – can make it infuriating. If every golf course is a minefield sown with potential disasters, we have to play the game in a state of mind which acknowledges that, ignores it, and, if disaster comes our way, puts it behind us. Emotional control is essential in golf.

Be excited about the game, but don't become angry with it. The ball isn't moving. The course is not going anywhere. If you are angry on the golf course, you can be angry only with yourself and you can't afford to be because you have another shot to play and you want it to be a good one. You know, don't you, that this time, the bounce may be in your favour! Forget the last shot, good or bad. It is confined to history. Get on with the next one. So, *never quit*, never give up. It's not over until it's over! One of the wisest thoughts about golf came from Harry Vardon when he said, 'Whatever you do, keep on hitting the ball.' Never quit before it's all over.

There are two worlds within one in this game. There is the business of striking the ball – the technical, mechanical business of swinging the club correctly with which we are all inclined to become obsessed. But there is also the business of playing the game, playing the course and of scoring.

The business of scoring is worth a good deal of thought even before we go anywhere near the course. Consider that big par five for example, the one that is straight away but just over 500 yards, with its only real hazards being bunkers on either side of the green – the one which somehow always gives you problems. You can drive the ball 225 yards and hit a fairway wood 200 yards. If you do that, two of these, two good ones, you are still left with a pitch of some 75 yards, a fair shot.

But hold on, consider this – you can hit a 4-iron 165 yards pretty reliably. Three of these would put you nicely on the green and there's no trouble in front of it, so why not? There is no law that says you must play a driver from the tee, a wood for a long fairway shot. Think about it.

What about that par four which needs a mid-iron second shot to a green which slopes away from you, from front to back, so that more often than not a perfectly decent shot will run over the back into the cabbage? Why not play short, short of the putting surface, a few yards short of the green? Then you would have a short pitch or chip, perhaps even a putt, with a much better chance of getting close enough to make the par four.

Of course, all of us are going to hit one or two loose shots, even bad shots in the course of a round, but we should remember Walter Hagen's saying, 'Three bad ones and a good one still makes four.'

Let's try a little exercise. Let's assume that your home course has a par of 72, arranged as four par threes, four par fives, and ten par fours of varying lengths. Five of these will be more than 400 yards, so they might be better described as 'par four-and-a-half'. Five of them will be less than 400 yards, so they might be better described as 'par three-and-a-half'. But no, let's still call them par fours.

If I said to you before you tee off, 'I'll give you pars at all the short holes', you'd take it! And let's say you play the par fives sensibly and cautiously and par all of them. Why, there you have eight pars already, without using a handicap stroke.

I'll say you make fives at all these long par fours, and fours at all the short par fours. You have scored 77 gross on the round. Even fining you three more strokes for the odd foozle, the putt which got away, and discounting birdies entirely, you are still round in 80. For all but the low handicap golfer that is a pretty good round of golf.

Of course, you've stayed out of trouble on this round and played damned well. But that is the object of the exercise, the reason for all that practice and thinking about the game – *scoring* is the name of the game.

So, don't just go out and play. Think about your course, and establish

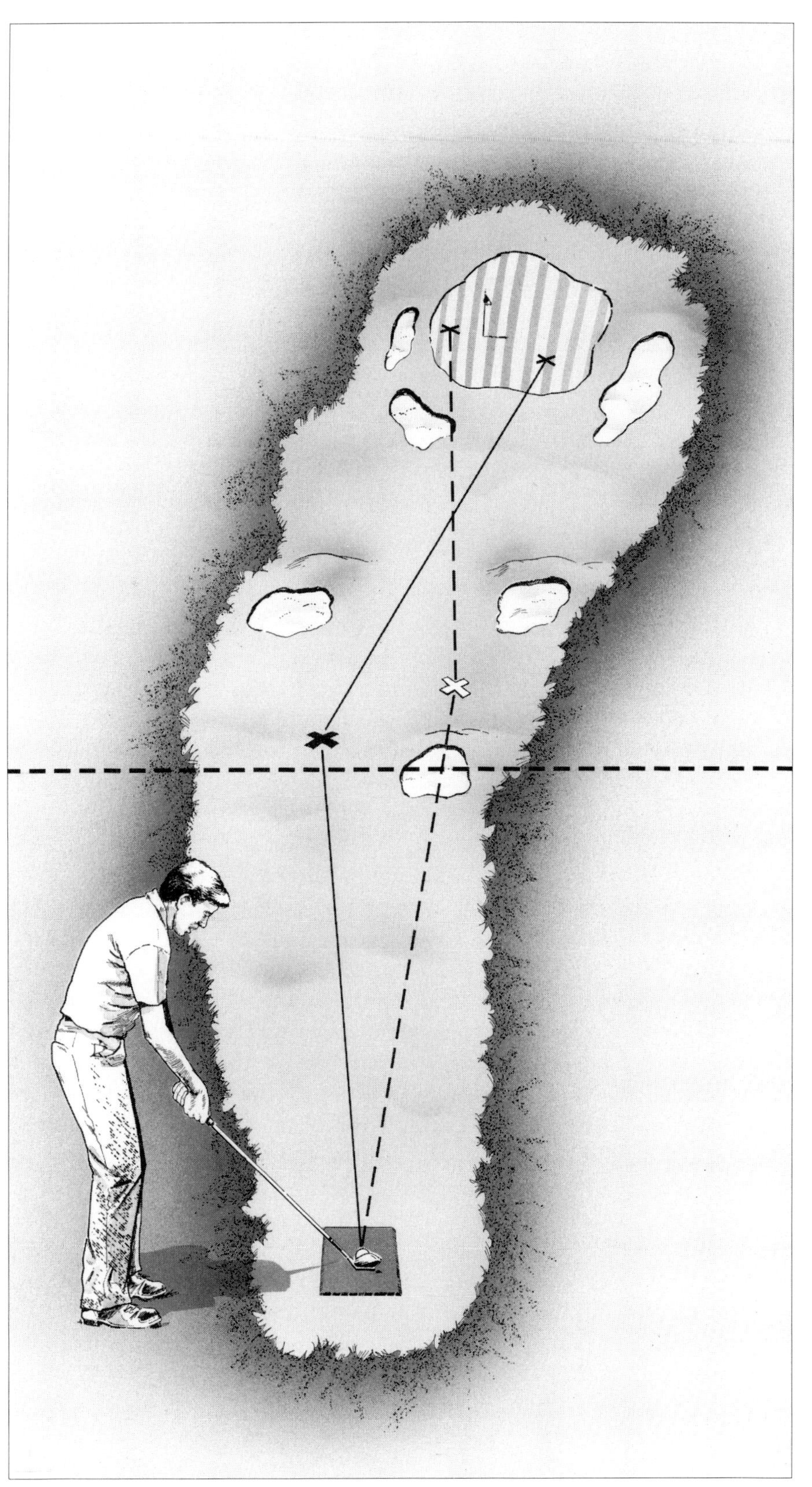

the risky route:
driver and 8-iron

the sensible route:
3-wood and 5-iron

the holes which you cannot reach in two, those long par fours. Play them as par fives and adjust your personal par accordingly. In a sense, you should be thinking from the point of view of each individual hole on the golf course. What is it asking you to do? What is its challenge to you?

It is a useful exercise to play the hole 'backwards' in your mind, from the pin position back to the tee. Is the pin position right or left, front or back? Depending on that, what is my best fairway position from which I can get an open shot to the green, to the flag? And if that is on the left half of the fairway, just past that left-hand bunker, how do I best get my ball out there?

Having got there, many players face another tactical dilemma in getting the ball level with the flagstick, or pin-high. Perhaps it is more psychological than tactical. In spite of the fact that almost all the trouble, i.e. bunkers, hazards, is in front of the green, or at the sides, most golfers are short with approach shots. Don't be afraid of that flag. Take one more club and swing carefully. In pitches, unless the ground is baked hard, shoot for the top of the flag. You'll be all right.

One of the most frequent and heartfelt cries in golf is 'Played pretty well – couldn't hole a putt.' This is a *non sequitur* – playing well includes putting well. Three-putting is the most scandalous waste of strokes in the game, and it doesn't really come from 'missing the short ones'. It comes from poor approach putting and the fact that you didn't get the approach putt close enough to make the next one a formality.

On all the long approach putts you should visualise a circle three feet in diameter around the hole. If you want to make that two feet, so much the better. Distance is the thing on these long putts – get it inside that circle! And if you miss from two feet, perhaps you deserve to drop a stroke. Oh, a hard man, that Alliss! This is another way of saying 'play the percentage shot'. If you become adept at getting these long ones up close to the hole, you'll be surprised at how many drop in!

Try always to play with players better than yourself. I know it isn't always easy to arrange but you can learn a lot from them in the matter of tactics; in noting how they play recovery shots; in how they handle situations on the course; when they chip; when they pitch; when they use a putter from off the green. Better still, watch the best tournament professionals – not only in the tournament itself but particularly on the practice ground. They hit the ball much harder and more skilfully than you ever will but there are lessons to be learned from them, particularly in the routine they have for the set-up, the stance and, above all, in the regular tempo of their swings.

In terms of the entire round, in playing the course and scoring, perhaps the best advice I can give is that you should concentrate *very* hard over the opening holes and *especially* hard over the closing holes, when you may be tiring. Above all, swing that clubhead with a single thought, whatever it may be, in mind.

Ace	American slang for a hole in one.
Address, or addressing the ball	A player has addressed the ball when he has taken his stance and also grounded his club behind the ball. In a hazard a player has addressed the ball when he has taken his stance.
Airshot	A complete miss.
Albatross	A hole played in three strokes less than par.
Angle of attack	The angle between the blade of the club and ball at impact.
Approach	A shot played to the green.
Apron	The closely-cut surrounds to the putting surface.
Away	The player whose ball is furthest from the hole is said to be 'away'.
Bandit	A player who scores persistently lower than his official handicap.
Birdie	A hole played in one stroke less than par.
Bisque	A handicap stroke given to an opponent who may use it at his discretion provided he declares its use before playing the next hole.
Blind hole	A hole at which the player cannot see the green or the flagstick when playing an approach shot.
Bogey	A hole played in one stroke more than par – an Americanism now in general use.
Borrow	In putting, the amount of variation allowed from a direct line to the hole to compensate for slopes on the green.
Brassie	The number two wood club.
Bunker	A hazard consisting of a piece of prepared ground, usually a hollow which has been filled with sand.
Caddie	A person who carries a player's clubs and helps him in accordance with the rules.
Carry	The distance from where the ball is struck to the point where it first strikes the ground.
Casual water	A temporary accumulation of water on the course which is visible before or after a player takes his stance. It is not a water hazard.
Chip	A short shot consisting almost entirely of run.
Closed stance	A stance in which the left foot is closer to the target line, from ball to target, than is the right foot.
Course	The entire area within which play is permitted.
Cross-bunker	A bunker which crosses the fairway, usually at right angles to the line of play.

Divot A piece of turf uprooted in the playing of a stroke.

Dog-leg A fairway which takes a pronounced bend.

Dormie As many holes up as there are to play, in match play.

Double bogey A hole played in two strokes more than par – an Americanism now in common use.

Draw A slightly hooked flight on the ball.

Drop Dropping the ball when permitted or required to do so according to the Rules of Golf.

Duck hook A shot which turns violently to the left without much height.

Duff A completely muffed shot!

Eagle A hole played in two strokes less than par.

Fade A shot that moves slightly from left to right through the air.

Fairway The stretch of ground, specially prepared, between the teeing ground and the green.

Follow-through That part of the swing that continues after the ball has been struck.

Fore! A cry of warning to other players or spectators.

Four-ball A match in which the better ball of two players counts against the better ball of two other players.

Foursome A match in which a team of two plays against a team of two, each team striking a common ball alternately.

Green The area prepared for putting.

Grip The part of the club shaft held in the hands, usually covered with leather, rubber or suitable material. Also, the actual grasp of the club by the player.

Gross score The total number of strokes played over a round, before deduction of handicap strokes.

Half A score on the hole equal to an opponent's score.

Handicap The stroke or strokes which a player is authorised to deduct from his gross score, according to his established ability.

Hanging lie A lie in which the ball rests on a downward slope.

Hazard A bunker or water hazard.

Hole The circular opening ($4\frac{1}{4}$ inches in diameter) on the green into which the ball is played! More generally, though, it's the area of ground between the tee and the green.

Honour The player or team entitled to play first from the teeing ground is said to 'have the honour'.

Hook To strike the ball so that it moves through the air from right to left.

Lateral water hazard A water hazard or part of a water hazard so situated that it is not possible or practicable to drop a ball behind the water hazard in accordance with the rules. It is usually defined by coloured stakes or lines.

Lie The state of the ball's condition on the ground, or the angle between the clubhead and the shaft.

Line The direction in which the player intends to hit the ball.

Links A golf course laid out on land behind coastal beaches.

Loft The angle of the face of the club.

Loose impediments Natural objects such as stones, leaves, twigs, insects, worm casts, etc., provided they are not fixed or embedded.

Marker A person appointed to record a competitor's score in stroke play. He is not a referee.

Match play A contest between players or teams which is determined by holes won or lost.

Medal Common usage for stroke-play golf.

Nassau A scoring system involving three matches in one – over the first nine holes, over the second nine holes and over the entire 18 holes.

Obstructions Anything artificial, including the artificial surfaces of roads and the sides of roads and paths.

Open stance A stance in which the right foot is closer to the target line, from bail to target, than is the left foot.

Out of bounds Ground from which play is prohibited – defined by stakes or lines.

Par In theory the play which would be made by a scratch golfer in normal conditions. It is decided principally on the length of each hole. Any hole up to 250 yards is a par three for men; from 251 yards to 475 yards is a par four; holes longer than 475 yards are par fives. Women's pars are as follows: up to 200 yards is a par three; 201–400 yards is a par four; and over 400 yards is a par five. Allowances in par may be made by the club committee because of unusual conditions or circumstances.

Pin-high The ball is pin-high when it lands on the green level with the flagstick.

Pitch To loft a ball into the air, or the actual shot.

Pitch-and-run A shot so played that part of its travel is through the air, part along the ground.

Plugged ball A ball embedded in the ground.

Preferred lie An alternative lie when a player is permitted to replace the ball because of the condition of the course or in winter weather.

Pull To strike the ball to the left of the target line.

Push To strike the ball to the right of the target line.

Rabbit Possibly a novice, but more generally someone who desperately wants to play very well, but cannot, and probably never will!

Rough That part of the course which is not tee, fairway, green or hazard.

Rub of the green The chance deflection of a ball in motion.

Run How far the ball travels after it hits the ground.

Shank A shot struck with the hosel part of the club (which joins clubhead to shaft) and not the face of the club. Also known as a socket.

Short game Chipping, pitching and putting.

Side A team.

Single A match between two players.

Sky To strike the ball with a higher elevation than required.

Slice To strike the ball so that it moves through the air from left to right.

Spoon The number three wood club.

Stance The player's position preparatory to making a stroke.

Stroke A forward movement of the club made with the intention of striking the ball.

Stroke play A competition which is decided by the total number of strokes played by the competitor.

Tee	The wooden or plastic peg on which the ball is placed on the teeing ground. Also, the teeing ground itself.
Teeing ground	The starting place for the hole being played. It is a rectangular area two club-lengths in depth, the front and sides of which are defined by markers.
Texas wedge	An Americanism for a putter when used from off the green.
Three-ball	A match in which three players compete, each playing his own ball.
Threesome	A match in which one player competes against two others forming a side, and in which these two players play alternate strokes with the same ball.
Through the green	The whole area of the course except the tee and green of the hole being played and all hazards on the course.
Top	A shot which strikes the top of the ball.
Waggle	A movement to and fro of the clubhead, using the wrists only, usually done in preparing to take a stance.
Water hazard	Any sea, lake, river, stream, ditch or any open watercourse. It is usually defined by coloured stakes or lines.
Yips	An inability to commence the putting stroke and/or to make a quick jab at the ball.

INDEX

Italic numbers refer to illustrations.

I

J

K

L

M

N

O

P

Q

R

S

T

U

V

W

Y

Colour photos

Black and white photos

Diagrams